# ASSERTIVENESS

## *A Life Changing Communication Skill*

Raspberry Press

Cheryl Fountain, BSW

*Assertiveness: A Life Changing Communication Skill*
Copyright © 2021 by Cheryl Fountain
www.cherylfountain.com

Published by Raspberry Press

Edited by Carol Fountain Cimini

ISBN: 978-1-7773105-0-9 (Soft cover)
ISBN: 978-1-7773105-1-6 (Hard cover)
ISBN: 978-1-7773105-2-3 (E-book)

First Edition: April 2021

# CONTENTS

# PREFACE

ASSERTIVENESS IS A COMMUNICATION SKILL; it is a mindset; it is also emotional wisdom. The mind-body connection is an important part of assertiveness that is missing from most assertive training courses. The body and mind have certain patterns that have been hardwired into our psyches from our experiences. When we understand how our body and mind work together and use this information to guide our assertiveness practice and guide our choices, we make more intentional choices, and create a life that has more emotional balance.

# PART I

## PATHWAYS TO ASSERTIVENESS

# CHAPTER 1

## BACK STORY

One of my friends went away on a holiday for a few weeks and I volunteered to take care of her plants for her while she was away. One mid-day afternoon, accompanied by my 12 year old daughter, I went to water my friend's plants. When my daughter and I walked into the apartment building, there was a young couple sitting on a bench outside the building. They were intoxicated. They seemed harmless, a couple of young adults having maybe too much of a good time. When my daughter and I walked back down after watering the plants, only the young male was sitting on the bench. He was approximately 20-25 years old. We walked past him. He got up and started walking after us. I looked behind us, and he increased his pace and started calling out loud, "I know you want it" while grabbing his penis. We started running towards our car. He started running faster toward us, and continually yelling while grabbing himself. We reached the car just in time. He was inches away from the driver side door before I shut and locked the door. We drove away. My daughter and I were frightened. We did not know what to do. We were both very shaken.

It was the middle of the day on a Sunday, downtown in a small community, outside a college, and we were watering plants for a friend. The building itself is occupied by many retired people and students, and the building is known as a centre for community events. This act by this man was something completely unexpected. The only thing we knew to do was to run. We ended up calling the police and they investigated. There were witnesses watching from a window of one of the houses on the street. The man was apprehended and arrested having other charges warranted against him.

The fear that developed in the moment the man was chasing us, and from the experience, was something that took both my daughter and I time to recover from. Experiencing that level of fear and being sexually accosted in a place that is normally safe prompted me to learn how to deal with that situation. I wanted to know what to do if it happened again. What if he had caught up to me or my daughter? What would have happened? I wanted to know what to do if he had. I never wanted my daughter or myself to face that level of fear again.

## Choice

I made a choice that day that led me on a path I did not truly know at the time. From this event, I sought out learning karate for self-defence. This choice of learning how to respond in a fearful situation was my first step on the path I chose to my learning about assertiveness. In this book you will see how assertiveness changed my life and how it can change yours. Through story, theory, and providing concrete tools, this book will teach you important aspects about living assertively that will support you in learning about and practicing assertiveness in your own life.

# CHAPTER 2

## KARATE

Being accosted sexually is a very physical event. Your heart is pounding, the perpetrator is looking at you as a physical object and not as a person, and your ultimate goal in the situation, whether you realize it or not at the time, is to get yourself to physical safety. Because of experiencing this level of fear, and because I had just barely made it to physical safety, I wanted to learn how to fight back if I needed to, how to keep myself and my daughter safe in a situation where someone is physically attacking me or her. I chose to learn karate.

### *Learning Karate*

I had always wanted to learn karate. When I was a child watching the movie Karate Kid I would pretend to be the karate kid for hours during and after the movie. My uncle taught karate and he told me I had a good kick which I remember made me feel good about myself. However, I never pursued karate until a few months after being accosted in my thirties. When I began karate I could barely do a single move. I felt I did not know anything, that I looked funny, and I would never get it. One of my first classes a Senpai asked me the reason I decided to practice karate. My answer was for self defense, and physical exercise.

It took me an entire year to rank up from white belt to yellow. This was not easy as I had to overcome my own self-doubt, I had to keep trying to "get it" even when I felt like I never would, and I had to learn to kiai. A kiai is a warrior yell, where you put your heart into your voice to deliver a loud noise while completing karate movements. It is used to shock your opponent and is also known as an expression of spirit. Kiai was very hard for me as I did not want other people to hear me. I mostly did not want to be heard because I spent a lifetime of not speaking up or from myself with most people. I found when I did speak up or from myself, I would be shut down or made fun of. Because of always being shut down or laughed at when being myself and or voicing what I wanted, I lost (or forgot) the courage to speak up, and I lost my ability to voice my wants. I learned to instead go with the group and say what I thought they wanted to hear. I made decisions based on what I thought would please others, forgetting about myself and my voice.

Another part of karate is learning kata. Kata is a series of movements that includes kiai. I learned to perform kata in front of people as part of the training. When practicing karate, although physical in nature, changes happen within a person as well. Karate is repeating similar movements and techniques as part of the training; practicing the same motions over and over again to learn the movements, to initiate them better each time, and to refine them into becoming second nature.

During the first year of karate, I let go of my self-doubt, I started to remember the movements, and gained confidence. The kiai became easier for me and in a way it helped me find my voice in life, outside of karate. When I first practiced kiai, I experienced an inner resistance from my thinking I would never be able to do this. Then my kiai progressed from just a thought, then a whisper, then a louder noise, into a yell. My kiai grew into visualizing myself punching someone while I yelled aloud. The punching was not out of hate or anger, it was punching out of power, in the spirit of protecting myself, my space, my voice, my right to be. Practicing vocalizing over and over again helped me kiai and helped me start speaking up more in life as well.

# CHAPTER 3

## THE BENEFITS OF KARATE AND PARALLELS WITH ASSERTIVENESS TRAINING

Karate is a form of assertiveness training. The mainstream focus of karate is the physical skill of protecting yourself and standing your own ground. As you practice karate, your mental state changes. Your confidence grows. Also there is a team-building environment karate can offer which fosters a healthy growing ground for confidence and self-esteem while at the same time learning how to apply tools and techniques in dangerous or challenging situations.

### *Confidence*

Confidence is one the biggest rewards of practicing Karate as well as practicing assertiveness that I have experienced over the course of my progression. At the early stage on my assertive path, karate gave me a confidence I had never known before. I was physically strong. I would open a door and it would swing very easily, whereas before it would take effort to move it. I knew how to kick, punch, and hold my physical ground. I was learning to throw someone and found my size is the perfect size to throw taller people if I got the angle just right. It was empowering. Also practicing kata in front of others, being able to remember kata, the continuous physical and personal development that occurred while I learned the movements and repeated movements over and over again, supported the development of my personal confidence. When you practice something often you become really good at it. When you are really good at something, apply it, and see the difference it makes, it is empowering and motivating. Not only was my confidence growing, when I practiced karate, I was the healthiest I had ever been in my life.

### *Team Environment*

The team environment of karate I experienced is one that supported my efforts to grow stronger physically and into my own confidence. In contrast to the friends I chose who took actions that resulted in my feeling I was not allowed my own voice without reprimand, the karate environment fosters a level of self-respect and respect for others. The kicks, punches, and throws learned are practiced with other people, and it is taught to be careful not to hurt others while at the same time knowing our own power and knowing the techniques can cause harm. The goal of karate is learning how to aim punches and kicks properly without actually hitting hard, knowing if you did hit hard how much it could harm the other person. It is learning a form of physical control that is challenging and also rewarding. When working with a partner in sparring or when practicing techniques, the partner usually responds with praise and encouragement. Both partners recognize the skill it takes to land a good point, and the effort behind learning how to exercise the skill.

Karate parallels the skills of assertiveness where there is a power in assertiveness that aims to score a point (get a message across, speak your mind, stand up for yourself) without hurting the other person or persons. The karate environment of encouragement, respect for self and others, self-growth and challenge, is assertiveness in spirit. Part of an assertive practice is the confidence and courage to encourage others. Be the voice of support. Share what you see that will make a difference in another person's life in a way that is respectful. Practicing assertiveness is also being that person who recognizes opportunities to support others, the community, the group, the moment, and the intention. Similar to karate, assertiveness is seeing the situation, assessing it quickly, recognizing what techniques apply, and utilizing techniques to get to your intention, while at the same time respecting others. In karate practice, you learn to use powerful techniques to respond to situations with the wisdom about how much power to apply and what timing to utilize, in order to successfully reach your goal, (scoring a point, escaping a dangerous situation), causing no intentional harm.

## *Responding to Real Life Dangers*

In karate it is taught that there are dangers and challenges in life. Karate was created as self defense, from a day when villagers had no military and required to defend their community from warring forces. Real life dangers exist. Karate teaches how to respond when someone is running towards you, punching you, grabbing you from behind, grabbing your hair, and many other threatening scenarios.

Knowing and acknowledging danger exists, and learning how to spot and respond to danger in a way that is wise and safe is also assertiveness. Like karate, being able to recognize threat, and move through the situation with confidence and intention despite how scary or emotional the situation is, is assertiveness. Standing your ground physically and verbally, with the support of mental strength and skill acquisition, is what assertive training provides.

## *You Cannot Control the Actions of Others*

Assertiveness is also realizing you cannot control the actions of others. I went to a self defense course separate from my karate training, after I had already begun teaching assertiveness training courses. It was said by an instructor that you can always recognize danger if you pay attention. I must say that this is not true. I do understand, and karate supports the theory that if you are more aware of your surroundings you are able to see and predict more of what is going on in your immediate environment. On the other hand, if someone comes up from behind you on a busy street and grabs your hair, is it fair to say you were able to see it coming?

It is not your fault that person grabbed your hair, that was not your choice, nor could you have done something differently to have prevented that person's choice. You could be walking down the street saying and doing nothing and someone could take offense with you and attempt to start a fight, chastise you, or demand you quit looking at them. You could compliment someone but they think you are patronizing them. In karate and in assertiveness training you learn to read body language signs to support you in predicting what someone is thinking or what they might do next, yet you will never know 100 percent because people have their own intentions, their own feelings, their own thoughts, their own patterns, and their own beliefs.

## *You Can Control and Choose Your Actions*

You can however control your own actions. Both karate and assertiveness are skill building practices that teach personal control and wisdom. Practicing similar actions repeatedly (physical, verbal, or mental) strengthens your ability to respond in the way you have been practicing. Assertiveness training teaches how to defend while not being defensive, and how to respond respectfully and powerfully to an attack without intentional harm. Even though there are times you might want to attack back, instead assertiveness training teaches how to respond wisely; how to speak clearly in a non-offensive way when someone has offended you; and how to speak up for yourself, respect yourself, and communicate with the other person that you deserve respect.

There are times when you need to yell, you need to scream, and you need to run. Learning to think clearly and move through emotions and make clearer decisions, no matter how intense emotions become, is an important benefit of assertive practice. Part of the assertive practice will be forgiving yourself when you are the person who took the compliment as patronizing, when you were the person who yelled at your kids because you had enough of them being loud, forgiving yourself when you misinterpreted a look or took personal offense at someone just walking down the street for whatever reason. We are human. We have defense wired into our systems and we do not act wonderfully all the time.

In the coming chapters, this book covers how people react from defense systems and how these defense systems are built over a person's lifetime and experiences. Karate also teaches to move past what are considered built in reflexes like wincing, pulling away, cowering, turning your back (which are reactive defense systems). In karate, when practicing to respond to things that might have activated these reactive defense systems, such as by leaning into them, keeping a steady eye, or backing away confidently while holding your ground, it is discovered that these reactive defense systems were just built up patterns from repeating them over time. As you practice new ways of responding, your reactions change. Changing patterns are uncomfortable at first but with practice people can change how they "naturally" respond to different events, and build new more effective defense mechanisms that actually support us. Training to respond differently and wisely reduces the feelings of victimhood because we know that we can do something and we have tools to respond. People cannot fully predict what other people will do. People can learn how to respond and control their own actions that supports what they want to attain in different situations such as getting out safely, standing up for oneself, expressing how one feels, or stating what one wants.

## *Approaching Assertiveness Like Karate Training*

When you are aware of tools to respond in different situations, and aware of how your own and other people's mental processes operate, you can respond with actions and techniques that support you. Similar to repeating a physical skill in karate practice, when you repeat mental and verbal skills, those skills become easier to use. The more you practice assertive skills, the more easy it becomes to move, speak up, and think clearly of how to respond in different situations. Also, the more you practice, the stronger you become at what you practice. Self-esteem and confidence naturally develop from being good at something and recognizing the difference your practice has made. When you have confidence and self-esteem you open the doors to new positive experiences because with confidence and self-esteem new challenges appear to be easier, you believe you are more likely to succeed, and you feel less fearful of not succeeding. Practicing using assertive skills and techniques as often as possible, in different situations, with different people will make those skills stronger. The more you utilize the skills the easier it will become to use them, to recognize when to use them, and you will be able to use them in different situations more easily.

This book covers multiple skills you can utilize. What I am asking you to do is approach assertiveness training like one would approach karate training. There will be times you only think of what you will say, or could have said. There will be times you can only whisper. There will be times you feel awkward, and believe you will never achieve it. The goal is to keep practicing, keep learning, take one extra step this time. If you did not quite get it the way you wanted, try a bit differently next time. With practice, time, and continual steps towards acting assertively, your courage will grow, and it will become easier.

Before we enter into assertive skills and mindsets, my personal story continues to share how the mind-body connection is an important part of our lives, and how utilizing assertiveness could support more healthy responses, even when we ourselves are experiencing poor health.

# CHAPTER 4

## HEALTH AND MENTAL ASSERTIVENESS

After three years of practicing karate, I chose to have another child. I was in the best physical health of my life, I had met a man I deeply loved, and wanted to share raising a child with him. Having a child is a very beautiful amazing experience. On the other hand, complications can arise that challenge the mother's and family's health. This happened to me, and events surrounding the birth of my son sparked me to learn the mental aspects of assertiveness, and eventually led to the classes I run, and the writing of this book.

### *A Time Supposed to be Full of Joy*

In my third trimester carrying my son, the company I worked for was restructuring the staff and I was assigned a new boss. The new boss piled work on me, increased my annual budget responsibilities from One Hundred Thousand to Two Million Dollars, and increased my working responsibilities by fifty percent more. There were other pregnant women in the office and as they were closer to their due dates and more uncomfortable in their pregnancies, their managers did not pile on more work, and instead started the process of easing their responsibilities to be focused on training other staff so their responsibilities were properly covered during their maternity leave. I had some physical complications and could not sit or stand easily at work, and the extra work piled on me was very stressful. I remember crying in the bathroom not knowing what to do. A co-worker came into the bathroom, she saw me crying and said, "This is supposed to be a time full of joy, one of the happiest times of your life," meaning my carrying and bringing new life into the world. This message has stayed with me.

I did not have the courage to talk to my new manager about how I felt, and I felt he was not an approachable person. I felt overwhelmed with emotion and discomfort. My physical restraints and pain became so bad I sought medical support, and my doctor advised I go on reduced duties. With letter in hand I had to talk to my manager about the doctor-ordered reduced duties and my discomforts. When I approached him he did not know how to respond either.

The discussion made him uncomfortable but he did not share this with words, instead he awkwardly shifted the topic. It was a difficult time and it could have been more emotionally and mentally comfortable if my boss and I utilized assertive techniques and opened up the conversation. He could have said, "Cheryl this conversation makes me feel uncomfortable" straight out instead of avoiding the conversation. I could have replied, "I am uncomfortable also." I could have also talked to him about my perception about the work load being piled on me while most people in their third trimesters with no physical complications, were having their workloads focused on training and preparing for their departure, instead of crying passively in the bathroom. It might have drawn his attention to what I was seeing, and it would have opened up the possibility for him to make different choices around the information, if he so chose. Looking back now, I see the increase in budget and increase in work as a compliment. It shows he believed I could handle it, and because I had not told him my physical discomforts he would not have known how I felt. At the time I did not see it this way. If I had seen it this way, or if I had talked to him honestly, this entire experience could have been different.

## *Dark Time and Illness*

After my son was born I did not heal well at all. I was not able to sleep and I could barely walk. The nurses at the hospital neither check on me often, nor checked on me physically to see if things were healing properly. When I was discharged, I could barely walk out of the hospital and nurses commented on it but no one checked to see what was wrong. I did not ask for help either, not realizing how sick I was.

Two days after being home, a home nurse came to check on me. I could still barely walk and I was in a lot of pain. The home nurse did not take my concerns seriously, despite me saying something does not feel right, instead she scolded me about co-sleeping with my child. Three days after the home visit I went to a doctor. The doctor did an examination and found material inside my uterus, remaining from the birth. She removed the material from my womb and told me to come back to the clinic or go to the hospital if I get a fever or have worsening symptoms. Due to worsening symptoms and pain, I went to the emergency room the next day, they sent me home not believing the level of pain I was in. I went two more days in a row, and was sent home each time. On the fourth day I again attempted a hospital visit for help, I broke out into a high fever. I was going septic. The doctor and nurses were scrambling to decide if they could do emergency surgery in the Yellowknife hospital or if I would need to be sent by helicopter to Edmonton, the nearest city that could deal with septicemia, blood poisoning.

I was out of it. I could not comprehend what people were saying and I was very confused. They decided to do surgery in Yellowknife. I was in the hospital for five days and symptoms kept arising. I needed to go back in to surgery and had a number of complications afterwards that continued a cycle of pain, including insomnia, scar tissue pains, anxiety, and on top of that kidney stones. I do not remember well the first month of my little guy's life, everything was a fog, I could lift him and breast feed him, but could barely do much else physically.

I had multiple signs of infection before it became so bad. I remember smelling something funny during the symptoms, and I even questioned if it was the baby who smelled bad. I was smelling my own infection. I could not walk. I was in constant pain. I was dizzy. I was beyond normal exhausted after giving birth. I saw other moms carrying their babies in a carrier at the appointments and I could barely lift my child even without a carrier. All of these signs and the doctors and nurses dismissed them. All of these signs and I did not fight for better help.

If people listened to me and believed me about the pain I was experiencing and examined me from the beginning of these symptoms, much of this could have been prevented. If I had listened to myself and trusted my body as it was telling me all was not okay, and if I spoke up more and insisted for help, much of this could be prevented. At the time I did not speak up beyond the nurses and doctors dismissal of my experience, as I felt they were the professionals and that something must be wrong with me as a person, or mentally, as I was in this much pain and they insisted I was okay.

## Being on Medication

After the surgeries I was placed on heavy medications. There was a lot of pressure from nurses to keep breast feeding through the process, causing my little guy to have stomach upset and irritability which added to the stress and trauma of the entire situation. The antibiotics destroyed my immunity and little guy received a portion of this through breast milk. Babies are building their immunity and gut flora for the building blocks of their life, that is their job, and mine had a steady instream of heavy antibiotics through me. The first three types of medications did not take away the infection. I needed more surgery and more stronger antibiotics. At the same time I was on morphine and codeine for pain.

The morphine did not work very well so I stopped taking it completely. It never took away the pain it just made things feel "okay" even though I knew and was very conscious that things were not okay. The morphine also caused a terrible fog and prevented me from being fully involved in what was happening around me. I could barely see my child let alone acknowledge him. It literally interfered with my ability to see clearly and experience my emotions about life. Things became fuzzy and foggy.

The codeine took pain away but completely changed my bowels where it became impossible to go to the bathroom. My entire lower area had already gone through so much trauma with child birth, a major tear in the perineum, and two surgeries, next came extreme constipation with nothing being able to pass, to finally passing something, creating a fissure, which took nine months to heal, and continued to be an issue for three years afterwards. The codeine also stole my ability to enjoy anything. It also created a form of fog.

I was on antibiotics for over six weeks, codeine for even longer than that, and then treating the fissure for over nine months. Anxiety coloured my interactions with people around me, my thoughts about life, my thoughts about my experiences, and my thoughts about being a mother again. I could not fully enjoy the experience of my beautiful baby son because I was in so much pain and so out of it. My personality changed, my health deteriorated, and I could no longer sleep.

## Not Sleeping

From all of the pain, medication, and building up anxiety, I stopped being able to sleep. It started when the infection was raging through my body when I was unware of the infection. The insomnia kept occurring even after surgeries, even when the medications given were meant to make a person drowsy. Instead the medications kept me up and created anxiety. My anxiety grew and I my inability to sleep became even worse. I could hear everything, almost like a super power of hearing, where if I had finally fallen asleep and there was the slightest sound in the house or outside, I would jolt awake.

I went weeks with less than fourteen hours sleep total in each week. Because I was breast feeding, doctors would not prescribe me sleeping pills. I was angry because the nurses were pushing me to keep breast feeding with morphine, codeine, and heavy antibiotics in my system but I was not allowed to have anything to help me sleep. Looking back, I was too out of it to realize I should have stopped breast feeding much earlier, no matter what anyone had said. It was not until I went three days in a row to the emergency room, again, having almost psychological break downs in the emergency room that a doctor finally prescribed me something safe for breast feeding that could help me sleep.

Even with the medicine it took me four months to start sleeping a little bit where I did not require using the medication every day to help me sleep and stay asleep; and it took four more months after that to never need the help of pills to sleep again. Near the end of my experience with extreme insomnia I had integrated magnesium citrate and coconut oil into my diet daily that supported my ability to sleep. Even then I would wake up to the slightest of noises due to anxiety and being a mother to a baby. To this day I need to maintain healthy practices to maintain my ability to sleep.

Sleeping issues is one of the most difficult issues to live with and it is not easy to fix. Each person is different. There are different causes to insomnia and different methods help different people try to sleep better. I chose to stop breast feeding about a month after I started sleeping a bit better, and once I stopped the breast feeding, my little guy slept much better too. The fog was lifting enough for me to realize I should have stopped breast feeding from the beginning because my body was creating breastmilk that was upsetting my little guy's body. I was too much in a fog to know this before, and there was a lot of pressure from the professionals and society to continue to breast feed. My husband had thought I should stop once I had the first surgery but I did not consider his opinion. Looking back I wish I did. If I had considered his opinion, and listened to him instead of listening to the pressure of nurses and society, I could have taken away some of the trauma and stress of having a colicky baby who was also irritable.

## *Illness Kept Happening*

I experienced illness and unhealthy sleeping patterns for one and a half years while I desperately tried to figure out what was wrong. I had continual pains in the lower region of my body. Not only did I have the surgeries, the fissure, the anxiety, the insomnia, I also had five kidney stones pass during the first year after giving birth, scar tissue pains in my perineum from the tear where I had to go in for injections to reduce the nerve pain, and chronic pain in the pelvic area. The doctors could not figure out what was wrong. I underwent a colonoscopy, the results came back healthy; a Computer Tomography scan, or CT scan, because the doctors thought I had a rare disease they would not tell me the name of so I would not look it up, and from the results was found out I had kidney stones; and I underwent Magnetic Resonance Imaging, or an MRI, to see how my bladder and kidneys functioned. The pain was not going away even though the stones were passed and the tests were clear. I thought I was losing my mind. I thought doctors believed I was losing my mind. My anxiety was high and I was acting like a crazy person, always in waiting rooms or hospitals and not getting any answers and not feeling any better. I was not me anymore. I thought I would never come back. My confidence was gone. My esteem was smashed. I was not a nice person to be around nor easy to deal with.

## *Snapping Out of It*

I had to snap out of it. When I was seeking help for my sleeping issues on one of my visits with a nurse practitioner, she mentioned a centre for postpartum anxiety. She wrote down the phone number and website onto a piece of paper and handed it to me. I had known about postpartum depression but had not heard about postpartum anxiety. The nurse practitioner assured me it happens and many of the symptoms I was experiencing are a sign it was happening. I called the postpartum centre. They listened to my story and validated my experience. This was the first time anyone fully believed me or had an understanding of what I was going through. This validation was the first weight lifting off my shoulders. They also recognized the grief I was experiencing. I was experiencing grief for the loss of not being able to experience my new born son in a healthy way. Their validation meant I was not crazy. It meant something was going on with me and I needed support.

## *What Was Learned*

From this experience I learned when you are sick, really sick, decision-making capacity is either taken away from you by others, or you might not be in a state of mind to fully understand what is going on. I did not listen to myself, nor could I hear myself. At first I tried to express how I was feeling but the people around me did not hear me and I did not have the strength to continue to fight. Assertiveness could have made the difference if I could have found a way to express how I was feeling, to express that I did not see people listening to or hearing me, and if I could have asked, "Please check me over and ensure I am okay." Part of being assertive is considering where someone else is at. If even one of the nurses listened to me and put herself into my shoes to think, "Hmm, she cannot walk out of the hospital, that is not normal, maybe we should check her before we let her leave." The nurse practitioner who helped me identify what postpartum anxiety was, was the first person to really listen to me, and this was one and a half years after my original health issue and surgery. She heard me, and she gave me information that further supported me. This information started me on the path towards health, being validated, listened to, and believed.

## *Core Alignment and Emotional Wisdom Training*

Seeing a bit of light out of the dark, I knew something had to change. There was a literal fog around me, and I saw only negativity, I was full of anxiety, and I was devoid of feeling love. I called my mentor Kate, with whom I had worked for years but had taken a break from. Kate as usual said, "You called at the perfect time." Her and another person named Kate were working on building a new module for the Core Alignment Program on assertiveness, and she asked if I would be the test client. I agreed, and am very thankful I did.

Going through the program supported me in learning about what assertiveness is, how it benefits me and others, and it inspired me to want to share assertiveness information and skills with others. The difference assertiveness was making in my life inspired me. I began researching more about assertiveness. The more I read, the more tools I discovered. After the program, the fog was lifted. I still had raw areas as I was still healing physically and mentally. However, instead of showing up in the world unintentionally undergoing a pattern of pain and reactive survival, I allowed myself to feel the raw areas and still show up in the world the way I wanted to.

# PART II

## ASSERTIVENESS
## AND EMOTIONAL WISDOM

# CHAPTER 5

## EMOTIONAL WISDOM

Emotional Wisdom is a term which covers an understanding of your emotional and physical responses and reactions, and how your beliefs, values, and memories, affect your reaction in different situations. Emotional wisdom is learning how emotions form, learning what triggers emotions, and is actively being aware of the emotional process so we can move through our emotions by responding wisely instead of reacting. It is also a set of tools to help you recognize and navigate your emotional experience and expression.

### *Patterns of Reaction*

I mentioned in the previous section I had undergone a cycle of pain and reactive survival. What is reactive survival? Reactive survival is a state of reacting to events in a way that is not conscious, and is instead based from feelings such as pain, fear, anger, lust, or a drive for happiness. Reactive survival occurs when our emotions consume us, when we forget that what we feel is not entirely who we are, and when emotion drives our reactions to life events and even the simple of occurrences. When we allow emotions to drive our events, we do not add conscious consideration about what we want to do or what we are doing it for. Every action we take is our choice, whether we are making a decision with or without our emotion. When you are conscious of the fact that choice is behind our actions, you gain the power to see how choosing differently will change your actions and outcomes. When you consciously choose to take action, and choose different actions that actually work for you, you can change your life.

When we are in deep pain, we more easily see the world as being the source of our deep pain, and we react with defensive and protective mechanisms, often not consciously. Protective mechanisms include actions such as lashing out, anxiety, crumbling inwardly, using silent aggression, or using silent submission. When we experience something that causes pain, our brain connects this experience with other times when we experienced pain from our past, or it connects to references or examples from society, to make sense of the pain. The brain then determines how to respond to this new situation based on that information. Even if you are experiencing a new type of experience that does not feel great and you start feeling pain, your brain will search out past events to determine how to act in response. It might reach out to a time when your parents yelled at you, when the people in grade three ousted you, or when your kindergarten teacher told you were colouring wrong. The part of your psyche that does this is the subconscious. Your subconscious mind looks for past events in order to manage recent events. It asks, "What worked for me when I was in pain before?" The subconscious finds examples of what worked before, compares some of the sensual data to the current situation, and picks what it thinks is the best solution to deal with this situation.

Because we are human and have lived multiple years experiencing multiple situations, and often times without any mental training, we have used the same patterns that worked for us when we were children, and carry those patterns through our lives even though those patterns were not mature or truly supportive in our development. The reaction patterns worked at the time for the age we were at. Tantrumming, yelling, hitting things, giving the silent treatment, using emotional manipulation, crying, hiding in our room, thinking and saying aloud, "You don't love me anymore," are examples of these patterns. These responses helped us as children, and when we continue to use these responses and they continue to work for us, our subconscious brain remembers their effectiveness, and will default to use these responses again, and they become reactions. When these reactions work, we create patterns of behaviour that we repeat over and over again that become unconscious reflexes when used enough times. Sometimes in reaction to a very traumatic situation our subconscious will grab what worked for us to keep us safe from that situation, and will continue to utilize that reaction in response to new stressful situations as it believes, "This is the only way to be safe."

Once we understand these patterns, we can make different choices and respond versus react to our life experiences. Assertiveness training paired with this understanding supports healthy change as assertive tools support more healthy constructive ways to respond. When we utilize healthy constructive responses more frequently this helps to build new patterns that are constructive and healthy. It also helps build a better more balanced life that comes from yourself based on what is real and relevant now, versus responding from past experiences.

## *The Emotional Process*

People also use emotions to justify their actions, "I was mad so I kicked the door." However, there is a different way to approach emotions that helps people stand up assertively. As discussed above, we as humans create patterns of reaction. Below is a breakdown of how the emotional and reactive process works:

1. **Trigger (Sensory):** In the environment there is a trigger. That trigger is a sensory item that was paired with a belief and meaning from our past, maybe once, or maybe multiple times. We are not always conscious which sensory item is a trigger. This happens in our subconscious and unconscious. For example, sometimes people see a spider and there is a connection to the collective unconscious that signals danger, and other times we see the spider and have had our own fearful experiences in the past that we remember and our subconscious screams danger.

2. **Emotional Feeling (Physical):** Once triggered, the body experiences an emotion associated with the trigger. This occurs in the conscious body. Some examples are increased heart rate, hyperventilation, and sweating.

3. **Meaning-Making (Mental):** Once the emotion is felt by the body, the mind wants to make sense of the feeling, and looks for evidence to justify the feeling. This occurs in the subconscious.

Part of being emotionally wise is to recognize the above emotional process and be aware of it. When we are aware of this process and accept this is how our consciousness operates, it helps us navigate how we act in the world, responding to our emotions versus reacting unconsciously. Where we can make the difference is first remembering this process, and by remembering this process when we are in the meaning-making stage we can make a conscious choice. When we are conscious of the emotional process we can assess what is real and true in the here and now to base our response versus jumping from non-conscious conclusions based on past patterns from which our brains have operated for years.

When we assess what is real and true in the here and now, we can choose differently, apply appropriate responses, and apply assertive tools to support our conscious action. When we choose differently, we start a new neural pathway, different from the subconscious reflex wired from the past. The new pathway looks at real-time evidence of what is in front of us, what we experience, and other information that will support how we choose to respond. When we respond differently based on real and true information and start making this our new habit, it becomes easier to consciously respond in the now, versus non-consciously reacting to the past.

## Reality Check and Grounding

Knowing from the emotional process outlined above that there might not be any relevant present reason for an emotion, there is a tool you can use whenever you are spinning in your emotion to help ground you and stop the spin. Follow the process below to support whenever you are in heightened emotion or experiencing ruminating thoughts:

Look in front of you, what do you see?
Name things you see aloud.
Turn around and face the other way, look at what is behind you, what do you see?

Name things you see aloud.
Turn around again, face forward and look at what is in front of you. What do you see?
Name things you see aloud.

Only look at objects when doing this exercise and if you see an emotional item during this exercise, for example a picture of a family member or an emotional event like a wedding, draw your attention to something more general such as the wall, a vase, a door knob. This exercise helps calm emotion, brings you back into the present, and helps you ground into what is real and true. The wall is real, the door knob is real. It offers space so you can re-look at whatever happened to send you spinning, with a calmer and more grounded perspective.

Another version of this tool is naming five things you can see, four things you can feel, three things you can hear, two things you can smell, and one thing you can taste. In the first grounding technique you look at what is in front of you (what you see presently), then you physically turn around to look at what is behind you (or figuratively looking at the past), and once again physically turning around to face what is in front of you (figuratively looking at the present), now moving into the future. This figurative action is grounding because often times people worry about what was, or what will be much more so than what is happening now.

The thoughts and emotions we experience are not always from things occurring right now, but are more often from things that have happened or we think will happen. By looking in front of you, you are pulling the reality of the now into your main focus, by checking behind you, you are realizing what is around you now instead of what was in the past, and the final turn and reality check is resetting your focus on what is here now, by looking again from where you started, in the present.

# CHAPTER 6

## EMOTIONAL WISDOM THEORY

Emotional Wisdom Theory is a psychological theory that has a unique description of how the psyche works as it supports a person's emotional wisdom. Emotional wisdom is a way to recognize and understand our emotions, and how they function in conjunction with our body and mind, and to utilize this understanding to choose how we show up in the world. With emotional wisdom we can shift our emotions, our thoughts, and our actions to align more with what we want to experience in the world. Emotional Wisdom Theory concepts are aligned with the emotional process described earlier in this book. Below we will go into a unique theory of the conscious, subconscious, and unconscious that is described slightly differently than main stream psychology, and is aligned with understanding how the mind works in a practical way, and aligned with a neuro-linguistic programming psychological approach. The concepts of moving away from and towards, what you focus on is what you get, and energy are also discussed below.

## Conscious, Subconscious, and Unconscious.

Many people view the unconscious in the terms of Sigmund Freud, where the unconscious is full of innate drives that are from our primal selves such as sexual drives, hunger drives, and life protective drives. In emotional wisdom theory, the unconscious is a realm where everything you have ever seen or heard is stored, even from the womb, and some people believe information in the unconscious is even stored from past lives. The unconscious also is connected to the collective unconscious that Carl Jung speaks of, where it knows information from the whole of humanity and even knows about universal rhythms, such as rhythms of our earth, planets, and stars. At a more grounded level, our brains are more vast than we yet scientifically understand. Our brain has more capacity than we understand. It is a wealth of knowledge and stores every piece of sensory information, from our five senses, and from other senses we no longer use or have forgotten to use.[1] The unconscious is also where the higher self, spirit, or soul lives. The unconscious in Emotional Wisdom Theory is akin to the superego of Freud's theory.

The subconscious is normally spoken of as equal to the unconscious, it is "sub" consciousness, or below awareness. In emotional wisdom theory, the subconscious is the ego. The subconscious is the part of our awareness that is the gateway to the unconscious. It is the thinking and reasoning part of ourselves. It picks up memories that help support the beliefs we have created about events, incidents, and accidents in life, such as connecting certain tones or sights to past memories, and gathers the information under our consciousness. The goal of the subconscious is to protect

---

[1] The Egyptians believed we had 360 natural senses!

us from harm. If it finds evidence that is aligned with one of our supporting beliefs, it relaxes and says, "Go for it!" The subconscious naturally recognizes information that supports pre-existing beliefs about experiences. For example, a person wants to quit their job but will not do so out of fear. This fear comes from the subconscious pulling information from societal norms and from past events that supports the belief such as: "Quitting a job will bring you misfortune," or, "You will fail," or, "You will not get another job," or, "The economy is bad. Do not quit your job." However, if the belief from past experience is that you have seen multiple movies where people end up in better situations when they quit they jobs, or you have seen your parents or other people close to you do well after changing jobs, your subconscious might be more supportive of your thought and give you permission to go ahead. You can shift what information your subconscious chooses to work from by consciously reviewing the facts of a situation, consciously shifting your focus onto more recent information that is relevant to the new situation.[2]

The subconscious' job is to protect you. It actually is your friend. It is the place we store beliefs and values, and from where we build our identity. This is the ego that many schools of thought talk about and ask you to shed. Building a relationship with the subconscious actually supports you in moving forward because it has supportive information for you. It very quickly pulls warning signs together to give you information based from your beliefs, past occurrences, and nuances from life. It digs into the unconscious memory,

---

[2] We often take from the past to worry about the future without looking at what is truly right in front of us. When we can start seeing what is in front of us with an un-biased view, we start seeing a new truth with less limits, and our opportunities grow. From there we build futures that we want, instead of continually living in our old patterns and only dreaming of what we want.

and the collective unconscious for you when you are going about your normal day-to-day activity to help protect you from harm.

When you work with your subconscious in a supportive way, it is a great information finder, and allows access to the unconscious. Building a healthy relationship with your subconscious includes learning about the processes of the subconscious, understanding what it is there for, and shifting your beliefs and values so it can act from a more supportive place on your behalf. When you get that feeling of fear, it is because the subconscious has found something. Sometimes the subconscious it is correct in sending you signals to feel fear, and sometimes it is incorrect. When you work with your subconscious, and remind it of your intentions and goals, it relaxes and helps discern with you what is real and true. It is important to value this part of our awareness and consciousness because it is a gatekeeper into the unconscious. Without the subconscious, it would be hard to be human and have an identity. It literally is the connection of our physical body and physical experiences, to our unconscious self, spirt self, or soul self. It is the connection of our physical being to our universal existence.

The conscious body is the physical form we are in and the physical things that we do. It is how we act and show up in the world. The conscious body includes our environment and the things that happen around us.

Of note, I also use the term unconsciously throughout the book. Unconsciously does not mean the unconscious; it means not acting consciously, such as experiencing a sensory trigger, reacting to it, but not being conscious of the sensory trigger being the cause. The trigger information is stored in the unconscious memory house, but the meaning of the trigger is decided by the subconscious. There is an unconscious part of the subconscious (where some of it operates with our not being conscious of it) and there is a conscious part of the subconscious. When we realize the processes of the subconscious we can say, "Oh there my subconscious goes again trying to find a reason," or, "There it goes again finding evidence for the negative." So when I use the term unconsciously I mean not being conscious or not being aware of.

## *Putting it Together*

Here is how the unconscious, subconscious, and conscious work together:

Someone asks you on a date. Your subconscious looks through the history of any date experiences in your unconscious memory bank, like a super computer searching through tons of data. It also checks what the word "date" means to you, and checks what a date with this type of person would mean based on media or other past information. It would assess how the person asked, or when they asked compared with community or social expectations, and assess all other information stored about being asked on a date. The subconscious then forms an opinion, normally in a state of feeling: fear, joy, excitement, nonchalance, and the subconscious pairs the emotion with any thoughts about accepting this date request. You feel the emotions in your conscious, in your body, and think thoughts based on this information, which then might enhance the emotion further. If your emotions are fearful and thoughts are stating, "No way, I do not like this person," or questions, "What would my mom say," the conscious part of you shows up by declining the invitation, or by completely ignoring the request. Or, maybe you would say yes even though you want to say no because saying no is even more scary than going this date.

Applying emotional wisdom concepts and tools with assertiveness training can support you in being more conscious in your choices. As you begin understanding emotional wisdom concepts you have more information to use in a supportive way, and applying your understanding assertively, you can use that information and act in a way that is right for you. For example, maybe dating was scary before because you had been rejected after a few dates, and you do not want to do that again. Yet this time you like this person and you are excited by their offer and there are no other warning signs, or red flags. You want to go but you are scared you will be rejected. Your subconscious is screaming, "Say no because you do not want to get hurt again," but you want to go. You can use emotional wisdom and assertive techniques with yourself to find out what is real here and now. For example, you can remind yourself or your subconscious that this is a different person, you know him well and you two have spent time together before and it worked out. You can ask yourself questions to help you realize what is true for you in this present situation such as, "If this person did reject you, what is the worst that could happen," or acknowledge this is a different situation and person therefore maybe it will work out. Also you can recognize things are temporary and even if there is rejection and you became really sad from it, the sadness will not last forever. These are truths, and when you show up more assertively in life, you see truths more often, because you are being true to yourself. As we project ourselves into our realities, when we are more often truthful to ourselves and embrace our full selves, we see more truths and live more fully because our reality mirrors our inner lives.

## *Moving Away From or Moving Toward*

Moving away from or moving towards are concepts to help you acknowledge when you are acting out of resistance or acceptance. It sounds simple. When you are moving away from something you are resisting it. When you are moving towards something you are accepting it. The concept is not quite that easy. You can think you are moving towards something, but at the same time actually be moving away from it. For example, when you focus on the reasons why you want to leave a relationship or a job, and start looking for a way out, you are not actually moving towards what you want. You are instead moving away from what you do not want. Your subconscious focus is to get away from the thing you do not want, you make choices around removing the item or situation, which means you are actually creating your decisions around and are focusing on what you do not want. What you focus on is what you get, and that will be discussed in more detail in the following section.

You can move toward what you want even if there is something in your life you want to change. How to do this is changing the focus of your subconscious. Instead of finding ways to get out of your current situation, shift your focus to find out what it is you want. Using the example of a relationship or job, ask yourself what it is you want in a relationship or job. Once you have a list of things that you want in these areas of your life, then start looking for opportunities to change in the spirit of attaining what you want. So instead of making choices around, "I need to quit my job," make choices around, "I want a job with a healthy work-life balance." This is now moving towards. Acceptance is not necessarily moving towards what you want. Acceptance is acknowledging things such as, "I am not happy in my current situation." It is acknowledging that other people do not change because of you, they can only change for themselves. It is also acknowledging when the challenges of a job have become too much for you, prompting you to want to change. Acceptance fits with moving towards what you want when you are accepting the opportunities, or are open to the opportunities, that align with what it is you want, and saying no to opportunities that distract you from what you want. Moving away from is resisting what comes up, and it causes you to take actions that will not give you the results you are looking for. It often continues a cycle of finding things you do not want, and perpetually keeps your focus on the negative, which interferes with your ability to see things that you do want. With understanding emotional wisdom theory concepts you can learn to consciously change what you focus on which then shifts yourself out of the pattern of getting what you do not want, and moves you into realizing your actual goals and the list of things you do want.

## *What You Focus on is What You Get*

Your mind acts as a GPS system. Where you aim your focus is where you will go, and will be what you see. If you focus on what you do not want or the negative, your subconscious will find evidence for the thought you are thinking that you do not want and the negative in your environment to support those thoughts. And this will be all that you see. For example if you focus on a belief such as, "I cannot get my point across with my spouse," you will find that in more situations you cannot get your point across with your spouse, and you will remember more strongly the times you struggled getting your point across. Your subconscious defaults to seeing information to support your belief. It takes a conscious effort to look for and change your focus, which is a form of internal assertiveness by realizing and stating what you want and taking action and expressing what you want within yourself. If you reframe your focus and move it toward what you want, you will see more of what you want. For example, if you reframe your focus from, "I cannot get my point across with my spouse" to, "I would like to be understood more often and experience more clear communication," you will experience more instances, and see more evidence, of being understood and having clear communication. Setting an intentional focus and remembering your focus will support you in obtaining more of what you want. Similar to a GPS, what you set your mind to, like setting a destination, is where your subconscious will drive you toward. It will see information to support your destination, and will recognize opportunities to attain your goal. This is why knowing and focusing on what you want is important. When distractions come up, you can assess if it aligns with what you want, or is on the path towards what you want. When you set your mind to, "I want more clear communication," your subconscious will support you and recognize opportunities to attain more clear communication, such as by noticing communication techniques for relationships, or by noticing proper timing to have a healthy discussion with your partner. Using assertiveness to communicate what you want adds to the possibility of actualizing the changes you want in your life. Once you have set an intention and you know what you want, you can ask your partner, "I really want more clear communication with you. In what ways could we work together to support this." By telling your partner what you want and asking for his or her input, you are giving your partner an opportunity to share in making the difference. Like a GPS, there are different routes you can take to get to where you want to go, or get to what you want. When you plug in what you want, the subconscious will notice the routes towards what you want and you can choose which ones you want to take. Assertiveness speeds up attaining what you want because you clearly define what you want with yourself and with assertive techniques you communicate more clearly with others. When you communicate more clearly with others it gives them an opportunity to rise up and support you on your journey.

Focusing on what you do not want is also moving away from cooperation, collaboration, and understanding of yourself and the world around you. When you focus on what you do not want in a relationship (where relation means how people relate to one another; and ship means a method of carrying people over the flows of life) the relationship will be something uncomfortable, and become something undesirable. Most if not all relationships have their problems. It is how people navigate through the problems that make or break relationships. This is where knowing what you want is important. Do you want this relationship? What do you want in a relationship? Does your current relationship show potential for developing the things you want in a relationship? What things would you like to see that would make your relationship what you desire? And also of importance, is your partner willing to participate in creating the qualities you want in the relationship? What does he or she want? When two people do not want the same things or if both persons are not willing to work together, that is a time when people might want to decide to end a relationship.

## Energy

Everything we experience, whether a thought, a feeling, or a belief, is an energy. Our body is made up of moving energy molecules connected together, that bounce off each other in an area, to form a person. Going through energy work like Reiki and working through visualization techniques, shifts energy patterns. There is an ancient belief system that energy gets stuck in us as blockages, and when we have energy blockages this causes patterns such as sustained fear, lack of energy, forms of depression, and anxiety, to name a few. We move away from the energy blockage by trying to ensure nothing touches the feelings we do not like to feel, which actually causes more experiences of fear, depression, and anxiety, and drains our energy. When we work through energy blockages, we release the blockage, and allow energy to flow through us again. How does this connect to assertiveness training? Firstly, it is information, and with more information we can make clearer choices. And secondly, it offers a new perspective to help reframe experiences that can assist in building your energy flow. With increased energy flow comes increased ability to move toward what you want. With increased energy, courage and self-esteem happen more easily, versus when you are stuck in a belief that keeps you moving away from what you want. Acting more assertively, a very tangible act and an objective measure, is also a form of shifting your energy, and a form of changing the neural connections in your brain. Each time you get a feeling, start considering it like it is an energy. It is not good, or bad, just an energy. Watch it, feel it, before reacting to it. See what happens.

*Assertiveness Practice and Emotional Wisdom Concepts*

Assertiveness practicing is not just about showing up in the world being respectful towards yourself and others while standing and speaking from your truth. It is information finding. It is discovery. It is questioning. It is finding and using the information that makes a difference and sharing that with the world, with the people around you, while also considering where they are at. It is a balance of understanding self-knowledge, knowledge of others, emoting, and exercising courage, compassion, strength, wisdom, maturity, and patience. It is work in a most beautiful way, and takes conscious effort. Emotional wisdom theory concepts and tools support this work.

# CHAPTER 7

## EMOTIONS

Now that you have some grounding techniques and understanding of the emotional process and emotional wisdom theory, let us now discover some emotions, what they mean, how they can look, and some of their consequences. Part of emotional wisdom is also understanding that words have been paired with emotions throughout our lives. To better understand how we respond is to discover and re-evaluate what different words mean to us. Emotions are also described by words. Each of us have our own unique understanding of what different words mean, and we each have our own unique emotional vibration or attachment to different words. We are going to explore the emotions of anger, sadness, excitement, lust, and happiness. As you read through each emotion ask yourself, "What does this emotion mean to me?"

## *Feeling of Anger*

Anger is a strong emotion that is often expressed with behaviours that society deems undesirable. Yelling, throwing things, calling names, punching, hurting others, are the more darker sides of anger, or the anger that most of us associate with the emotion. There is a lighter side of anger. Anger is also motivating, it is a sign that there is something going on that is against your beliefs, values, self-identity, self-esteem, and it provides a drive towards change. The energy of anger when used properly is transformational. Assertiveness training allows people to experience their anger and at the same time use it for a higher benefit. When you express your anger in an assertive way, you get your point across as you express what it is you want to change. Acceptance that you cannot change others' behaviour, can support you when working through anger.

People use anger to get results, and after utilizing anger if the situation does not change in the way the person using anger wants it to change, the emotion can escalate. When you realize anger can be a tool, and maybe the tool is not working in a situation, you can choose other tools to help you get your point across. Anger is not obsolete nor an identity. If you shift your understanding of anger being an energy of motivation for change, you can step out of the emotion and find a better way to communicate towards a more positive outcome, instead of how most use anger as a weapon.

Anger is normally not expressed because we are taught that anger is a "wrong" emotion. It makes you "bad." Holding in anger creates an internal strife and can even develop into illnesses in the body. Remember the energy blockages described earlier? Heart attacks, strokes, and other cardiovascular illnesses are linked to internal anger.

Holding in anger also leads to expressing oneself through passive aggressive and passive behaviour. As you move through this book you will learn more about this process.

Anger also drives societal change. Women grew angry from not being able to vote. Women used their anger constructively, formed a movement, and would not stand down. From this they earned the ability to vote. First Nations groups in Canada were angry that their land was taken away and the Government refused to honour their title to land. First Nations groups took the Government to court which opened up the lands claims negotiations. Without their anger, they would not have been driven to do this. First Nations groups and environmental groups across North America are angry about how the planet is being abused and protest oil and gas development. They group together and stall oil and gas production. Without the drive of anger toward wanting change, and without their combining that drive with assertiveness, they may never have harnessed the courage to have their voices heard. Assertiveness is communicating clearly and respectfully, and when people tap into the courage that anger provides, people are enabled to speak out about the information that makes a difference to them, clearly, and loud enough for the unaware to hear. Again though, the people who hear choose what to do with the information; they cannot be forced to take action or believe what they hear.

When working with emotions I created a scale to support the understanding of each emotion. Each emotion has a good and bad side so to speak, or as I formulated a constructive and unconstructive side.

## *Anger Scale*

| Unconstructive Anger | Constructive Anger |
| --- | --- |
| Hate | Courage |
| Violence | Drive Toward Change |
| Condemnation | Energy |

These are no longer opposites on a scale, but a contrast of values. When you feel hate ask yourself what are you really angry about. When you feel anger ask yourself, what do you want to change. When you act in violence, ask what are you hurting about. When you are angry ask, how you can use this energy that will benefit you and those around you.

## *Feeling of Sadness*

Sadness is one of the emotions that people do not want to feel because in our society it is seen that if you are sad something must be wrong and sadness hurts. It is this deep feeling of pain that swells up inside your body, that puts pressure in your middle section all the way up to your throat. I can be so sad I feel it in my entire body. It can feel very heavy. After expressing sadness it can feel so much lighter afterwards, like a shedding of much heaviness. Sadness is a heavy energy, and once that moves through you, it lightens you.

Because sadness is so heavy it can be hard to let it move through the body. A lot of people hold onto sadness as it hurts so much it is hard to let it pass. Crying helps move it through. Some people hyperventilate. Some people hold their breath and hold back their tears. There is a cycle with sadness that can occur when you no longer feel normal unless you are feeling sad. People can become identified with sadness. I have become identified with sadness. Depression is a name psychologists give for chronic sadness, and many of my family members, especially the women in my family, have experienced a time of depression at one point in their life. When people are in this perpetual sadness they sometimes give up on trying to feel better and end up doing little to support any other emotion. They might stop bathing or eating or doing things they enjoy. I spent a long amount of time in my life very sad about the world, life, and myself. I was in this perpetual negativity, seeing the world similar to Eeyore in *Winnie the Pooh* where even if it was a sunny glorious day having a picnic with loved ones I could find something to be sad about. I had to learn and train myself to look for and recognize the positive things in life, starting small such as noticing a beautiful flower, recognizing I had food on my plate, recognizing I was a mom to an amazing daughter (and now a son too), and with support through coaching and from some very good friends, I stepped out of the cycle of sadness.

Although I stepped out of the cycle of sadness, I still feel sadness often. Sadness is a normal emotion that all humans experience at one point or another. It is a natural part of the human experience. I am still sad about some of the things that go on in the world, however I learned to disassociate myself from ongoing sadness. I accept sadness as a fluid emotion like other emotions. Some parts of life are sad and other parts are not.

Sadness can also be beautiful. Being sad about people hurting each other shows one cares about people and knows there is a different way. I get sad about how some children are treated, about children who are starving, and other world issues that affect the health and wellbeing of us all. If people are suffering it affects us all, whether we notice it energetically or not. Being sad about these things is beautiful because it shows there is heart and compassion for fellow humankind.

Things also happen directly to us in life that brings sadness. The death of someone we love, losing health, losing a relationship, losing a cherished item that belonged to a loved one. Sadness is an emotion of loss or injustice (which is a loss also). Sometimes even when something good happens there is also a feeling of loss of what occurred to get you there. Sometimes when something good happens it brings tears to us, which are known as tears of joy. Tears of joy are a recognition of something hopeful coming to pass in actuality, a mixture of sadness and joy. It is remembering the loved one who died and remembering how beautiful they were and are, and knowing although they have passed they are okay. It is coming through the other side of a health issue, knowing all you endured, knowing others are facing the same illness, and there is and was suffering, and there now is light and health. It is also knowing you will die and coming to terms with it, and being sad about the oncoming death, and also at the same time appreciating the life you have and still have, and the small things while your last days are upon you. Sadness is a beautiful emotion because it is the emotion of the heart. It is also beautiful when someone is able to express their sadness and another expresses their compassion for them. Sadness can bring people together in expression of common understandings, insights, and truths.

Society sees sadness as one of the undesirable emotions. People hold in their sadness or expression of sadness to try to hide their true feeling in fear that other people will either give them too much attention, think they are weak, will worry about them, or will catch the sadness. According to our social norms, if someone is sad it must mean something is wrong. Expressions of sadness can be seen as disturbing, such as if a person wails in public about a loss, others will feel disturbed and might turn away, while others may turn toward the crying person and ask, "What is wrong" or, "Do you need help?" In our society it is thought men are not allowed to show sadness or they will be seen as weak. Let us be honest though most women and men do understand and welcome male expression of sadness, and sometimes women and men still attack men for showing sadness. The paradigm is changing, however the old narrative still plays out where in male culture men are told to suck it up, to be a man, to not cry because men do not cry, and to be strong because being sad means you are weak. It is thought you are acting like a baby when you cry. In reality we all need to cry. It is a physical and emotional release of hormones, of fear, of anger, of tension, of frustration. Babies cry for simple things; adults cry for much bigger things and sometimes smaller things. Holding in sadness causes tension, hurts in your heart, throat, and other areas in the body. Arthritis is thought to be a form of holding in sadness.

## Sadness Scale

| Unconstructive Sadness | Constructive Sadness |
| --- | --- |
| Depression | Compassion |
| Physical Ailments and Pains | Honoring Truths |
| Debilitating Grief | Grieving and Still Living |

## Feeling of Excitement

Even within our more positive emotions and experiences we have patterns of reaction. Often times people do not think through more positive feelings thoroughly because emotions considered positive are also considered desirable or good. Even with more positive emotions there may be some reactions that have worked for us that do not create the results we want. For example, when I am excited about something, I feel nervous. This nervous feeling makes me feel ill, and I have physiological responses such as stomach upset, and feelings of high anxiety. Anxiety and excitement are very close emotional states in regards to physiological expression. Have you heard of the phrase "positive stressor?" Positive stressors are events in life such as getting married, having a baby, and starting a new job. They are socially expected to be positive experiences that also bring on stress. When I feel excitement, because it is close to anxiety, my subconscious exclaims, "NO! STOP MOVING FORWARD!!!" Because of this, for years I would stop moving forward. I was so fearful of moving forward because unconsciously my subconscious believed that to keep me safe from these feelings I must not move toward them. My body literally was telling me through heart palpitations, nervousness, and anxiety that if I do that exciting thing it will hurt me. In reality it was a misunderstanding by my very protective subconscious. My subconscious was trying to keep me safe from something that was exciting me. I did not know ANY of this as I was in a reactive state of survival. Reactive survival is feeling a feeling and allowing that feeling to drive what a person chooses to do. Once I learned how the subconscious operates, and how close anxiety and excitement were on an experiential level, I realized I was misinterpreting excitement as anxiety because it feels very similar. With this information, I could consciously think about what was really happening and ask, "Is this something that will hurt me or am I excited." Because of this realization, now when I experience excitement I can move forward. The understanding that excitement and anxiety are close feelings helped free me from my own imprisonment, and is how I was able to move forward with writing this book, with running workshops, and building platforms to deliver information that will support people.

## Excitement Scale

| Unconstructive Excitement | Constructive Excitement |
|---|---|
| Feeling of anxiety | Recognition of Challenge or Change |
| Taking Risks That Might Harm | Taking Risks That Might Support |
| Not Thinking Clearly | Trusting the Excitement and Intuition |

## Feeling of Lust

Lust can feel really great or really terrible. Often times people who are in the beginning stages of love are really in the lust stage of love. When experiencing lust, there can be joy all around you, colours are more bright, life is more exciting, you think this person is going to bring you the world, and he or she is the ticket to happiness. The emotion of love is a very powerful emotion and it changes over the course of our relationships. Love for a child is different than love for a spouse. The love for a spouse which we first experience changes as the years go on. It can become less exciting by natural progression as it is no longer is new, and you learn of all your and your spouse's less attractive qualities, never mind adding the discovery of each other's bodily functions, and changes we go through as we age and grow. Even if we deeply love the person we are with, the first stage of most relationships is experiencing the emotion of lust.

The emotion of lust is so motivating that we can stay up late at night with this person and wake up early in the morning on work nights and not let the lack of sleep bother us. We can go without eating. We create so much time for this person because we want to swim more closely to the feeling of lust. The sex is so good. Sometimes we skip work, sometimes we ignore our children, sometimes we are not yet divorced and are having an affair with the person we "love" or what I call lust.

Another indication to know our experience is lust is when we quickly fall in love with someone we do not really know. People go through stages in a relationship where love develops over time. The initial lust is the hook, similar to a drug, as it is powerful emotionally and physically. We have more energy, a renewed sense of life, future, and hope. We feel good about ourselves mentally and physically. May people proclaim in the lust stage: "This person is my soul mate!" All these things are beautiful and have a wonderful place in our lives, and are the beginning of something with good potential.[3]

What happens when you believe you found your soul mate? Your subconscious says, "This is good! This is rare! Jump on this!" (maybe literally), and because the feeling is so good and so positive, it drowns out other beliefs and information without consideration of certain consequences. The subconscious colours the experience by either building the understanding from a cultural understanding of love, which we learn from movies, and fairy tales, or from needs and desires from when we were little. An example

---

[3]  Not everyone experiences the beginnings of love this way as many cultures have arranged marriages or other patterned beginnings of relationships. I am speaking from experiences from a North American culture, from what I have seen around me, and the people I have met. Everyone has different experiences, so yours are yours and are not wrong if they are different. This concept of lust though is an insight of mine that I think will support people when experiencing these feelings.

of a subconscious narration would be, "This person feels so good. They will love me. I cannot see any evidence this person would hurt me because they feel so amazing. This person will not abandon me. This person will make my life better." What a promise! And the subconscious approves this relationship based on these thoughts, and then aligns with your feelings. When thoughts and feelings align, it is an energetic go ahead from two important aspects of yourself: the conscious and subconscious. When you experience this alignment of thoughts and feelings matching, it gives you certainty and confidence, whereby you take more certain action towards what you are experiencing. This is lovely! It feels easy and it feels right because of this alignment. Even if some wisdom comes through from your unconscious such as, "You have just met him," or, "He never talks about his life," you ignore that wisdom because two strong aspects of yourself are in agreement. The goal to alignment is to have your conscious, subconscious, and unconscious in agreement. When these three aspects of yourself are aligned it makes it possible for you to show up as the strongest you.

As time goes on, the feeling of lust lessens, and your subconscious starts recognizing different information and the narration changes: "Oh no, this person is not as into me as before. They are going to leave me," or, "She is not making extra time for me anymore, she must not love me." This is a stage of love where working with the subconscious to find out what is real and true will support you. Finding out what is real and true is also where assertiveness comes in. Being assertive means communicating when it is tough to do so, such as inquiring, "Hunny, we have been together for six months and we do not stay up late together anymore." Bringing up your concern utilizing assertive communication will give your partner a chance to explain how she or he sees the situation and will address the accuracy of your internal narration. She might reply, "Well Hun, I find going to bed at one in the morning is too late for me to sleep well enough for work." The response informs you the change is not about her not loving you, it is a reality that staying up can interfere with daytime responsibilities. The lust period is a high energy period, running a marathon of bliss, and as with any high energy period, there realistically and physiologically needs a period of balance, rest, and a break from heightened emotions, be they positive or negative emotions.

Being assertive is also reminding yourself of the information that will support you when your subconscious brings up thoughts based from fears. You can gently remind your subconscious with the information from the conversations you have had with your spouse, "See subconscious, she does loves me. She is tired and we had a great time staying up late for six months. Now we both need to rest, so we can move towards bigger and better things together, which when you have more rest can be more possible."

Understanding lust can also support people who are considering some more socially frowned upon choices such as having an affair or dating your boss. When your soul mate is married, or you are still married, and you found your soul mate outside of the marriage, or if your soul mate is in a position of authority over you, you can remind yourself of the physiological pull of the emotion of lust and tell yourself that there are other things you are not seeing now because of this feeling. Giving the situation time before jumping in propelled by your emotions, might help you from jumping into a complicated situation, and over time you might see how it will or will not really work for you. Giving it more time will support you in considering the financial consequences, the way it affects children involved, the reputation consequences, and any self-relation or self-esteem consequences. However, affairs outside of marriages or having relationships with persons of authority are complicated situations. Many people in these situations cannot see the consequences until much later, and many live with the consequences, learn from them, and grow from them.

## Lust Scale

| Unconstructive Lust | Constructive Lust |
| --- | --- |
| Not Thinking of Consequences | Experiencing Enhanced Energy |
| Not Seeing Full Information | Having a Lot of Fun |
| Running Wild With Beliefs | Running Wild With Beliefs |

## Feeling of Happiness

Happiness is the one emotion we all reach for. People actually go into a lot of pain thinking that they are not happy, and sometimes go through a lot of painful and fearful things to gain happiness. *I will be happy when* is a classic belief people follow and they strive to great heights either to find a relationship, to buy a big house, or to land a great career in search of happiness. Often times when people fall into the belief cycle of *I will be happy when*, the happiness experienced when they get what they believe will give them happiness is similar to how lust is experienced. When you reach happiness, it is joyous at first and all the images and sensory stimuli supporting the pros of the situation are seen and the cons are not seen. Then, over time, the person realizes that they are not happy again.

Many different books and motivational speakers will say this realization happens because you are not truly happy, that you need to go into yourself and change your beliefs about yourself or start loving yourself. Yes, changing your beliefs about yourself can support a more regular happy outlook, however I want to challenge this position as there is more going on here. Similar to lust, when you fall in love with an idea, such as, "If I had a relationship I will be happy," you become convinced it will make you happy. The information you have about what the relationship looks like, or the idea that you believe will make you happy, is different from the information you have when you actually attain the relationship, or what you thought would bring you happiness. For example, if the relationship you attracted ends up having challenges that you do not feel happy about, it will look different than the relationship you dreamt as it was supposed to bring you happiness. Challenges are not normally part of a persons idealized relationship. Over time once you have that relationship, or job, or house, or money, your beliefs about its value changes as you gain more information. When your spouse snores and does not like to help with dishes, your house has leaky pipes, your career takes all of your family time away, people always ask you for money and nothing else, your happy barometer changes and switches to frustration, sadness, and doubt. You then begin to think that you need a different relationship, job, house, or more money to fix this feeling so you can be happy again.

Similar to lust, after the marathon of happiness is run, there is a natural down time. There is a natural down time to any heightened emotional experience, and when your body and mind experience heightened happiness and elation, physically your mind and body require a bit of rest. Then other emotions and beliefs have more room to step in during that down time when you are resting. When you have thoughts such as, "I am not happy any more, something must be wrong," you look for something that is wrong and start focusing on that. When you focus only on the information that does not make you happy, this then becomes the focus of your attention. Your subconscious then connects the information with your naturally occurring energetic down, and then you believe you are no longer happy because of the new focused thoughts and your experience of feelings and lower energy align. The elated feelings are gone, and you reason that something must have changed and something is now wrong because you do not feel the way you did before. Alignment is powerful in both ways, when negative thoughts and feelings align, and when positive thoughts and feelings align. That is why it is important to align all three parts of your psyche. Adding the unconscious into your alignment adds the truth of situations as the unconscious knows what is true to you and has access to all of the information relevant to the situation including from your heart and higher self.

New information normally does surface about the situation you are happy about that may change how you view your experience. The truth from this experience is often that the situation that made you happy did not change, it is your focus that has changed from the more positive aspects of the situation onto to seeing less positive aspects. All situations have positive and negative aspects. To have one thing, sometimes you have to sacrifice another thing, for example usually having a career means that people have to sacrifice their time with their family to be successful at their career. Then it becomes a question of what you want to prioritize, or change how you do things in both areas of your life to try to have both a successful career and quality time with your family. If you become conscious of the natural process whereby you start noticing when the down times from experiencing elated happiness are in effect, you can choose activities to support focusing your mind on what matters to you and realize that you have not lost your happiness. You are resting naturally from experiencing heightened emotion and feeling happiness more profoundly will occur again.

## *An Exercise for Realizing Happiness or Change*

Here is an exercise to support when you think you are no longer happy. This will help you determine if you still want the situation you are in or if you want to make changes to the situation. To outline how to use this strategy, the following example will be utilized: You bought a big house and you were so happy. It developed leaky pipes and you are no longer happy about your house.

Step 1:   Remember why you chose the things you chose. What you chose something for is normally still true. For example, you may have chosen a big house with a yard so your children could have room to play, and your children freely playing brings joy to both your children and yourself.

Step 2:   Do a Reality check, which includes assessing information that is true to the situation. For example:
- Leaky pipes happen to anyone.
- House maintenance is a part of owning a house.
- Overall the rest of the house is great condition.

- Your children have their space to play, and you have your space to relax or play with the kids when you want to.
- There are financial costs to fixing the pipes but financial maintenance costs are part of home ownership.

**Step 3:** Take your reflections into action. Focus on what makes you happy about the house and take action to support that vision. For example, to support liking your house, take actions to have the pipes fixed, clean up the mess, and repair any damage.

This exercise can apply to anything in your life that upsets you when your position about something has changed and you feel you are no longer happy with the things you have attained and had previously wanted such as, your house, your relationship, and your job. There are times new information arises about something you once were happy about, that contradicts what you chose something for, or there is something that occurs that you will not tolerate in a situation. When you do the exercise above, the information you gain can support you, and after reviewing your answers, when you move through Step 3, the take action part of this exercise, you might decide to chose or do something completely different. The exercise is to support you in either keeping or making new choices that will support you. Below is an example of how I have used this in my life, when I had moved to the Arctic, lived there for 17 years, and was no longer happy there:

**Step 1:** I chose to move to the Arctic to support my boyfriend's career.

**Step 2.**  We no longer are together and I do not enjoy living in the dark and cold.

**Step 3:**  Time for me to move out of the Arctic and move to a place with more sun and warmth.

The lesson here is that if you focus on what you do something for, or remember why you have chosen something, it will support your memory of what you wanted in the first place and you can affirm if that is still true for you. Sometimes this in of itself is enough to bring a person back to a state of appreciation and happiness about the situation. When you do the reality check and new information surfaces that might tell you that you are actually not living what you want, you can then use this information to take conscious action and make new choices towards what you now want. When you focus on taking action towards realizing what you want, options occur that support you in ways you could never have created yourself. It is like something hears you and supports you in realizing what you are focusing on.

## *Chasing Happiness*

People chase happiness as if it is something to possess. Happiness is an emotion. Emotions are fluid. Emotions change. Emotions are not who you are. There was a time in my life that my baseline was happy, or rather content. It was not a glowing high energy joy for life that many people chasing happiness are after. It was a realization that things were going well, that I was making choices and realizing my choices. When my choices proved to not meet my intentions, I would change my choices and aim toward something else I wanted. I still felt fear; I still felt pain; I was still sad at times; and I also had a lot of fun. It was the most balanced time in my life where I enjoyed the moments I was in, and aimed toward changes to better myself and my life.

That balanced part of my life changed with a decision to have another child, and from my story look how a decision can change your life, and how information you did not, and could not know can make such a difference. I always wanted to be writer since I was a little child, but nothing pushed me to write a book before. The information and experiences I gained from that one decision, to have my son, were a life changer for me. My experiences around this decision pushed me to act and inspired me to write a book. I am realizing a childhood dream. I too am chasing happiness. I am chasing giving information to people that will support them in learning more about what happiness truly is, what emotions truly are, and how to work with emotions to enable people to have more emotionally balanced lives. A life where choices are visible options, and when the options chosen do not work as wanted, there is an understanding and realization that there are more choices to be made that will support building the life that the person wants.

*Happiness Scale*

| Unconstructive Happiness | Constructive Happiness |
| --- | --- |
| Chasing it Like it is Something to be Had | The Feeling it Gives Us |

# CHAPTER 8

## CHOICES AND EMOTIONS

Choices we make and how we make them affect our emotional process. There are components to decision-making that we are not conscious of. Being conscious of your choices and emotions supports a more balanced life. Utilizing the information shared in this book, when emotion steps into your life around your choices, you now have an understanding of how emotions work and you have some tools to help reframe your experiences and support your choice-making. The tools and understanding allow you to refocus on what it is you are doing and choosing, while at the same time experiencing your emotions. In the following paragraphs I present more tools to support your emotional wisdom.

### *Intention Setting and Being Clear on What You Want*

We set intentions often without really knowing we are setting them. The trick to more conscious and balanced decision-making is to start being conscious of what you are doing things for. Knowing what you are doing something for will support you in making a decision, maintaining that decision, and adjusting the decision when required. Below are questions you can use to support basic decision-making, and to discover what you are doing something for. The example of the buying a house that was used earlier in the book is utilized to illustrate how this tool can work.

**What is it that you want?** *I want a big house so my children can play, with a large yard so they can play safely outside.*

**What do you want this for?** *They need a lot of space to set up their toys and to be able to play without adults telling them to be quiet all the time. I want my own space so I can write, or do my own thing, but still have the option to play with them. The large yard is so they can play outside without me having to be there all the time, so I can do things alongside them, and they can play safely. A large yard will also give me a place to set up a garden a relax on evenings or summer days.*

**What are foreseeable benefits of this choice?** *More space for everyone in the family, more opportunities to go outside.*

**What are foreseeable consequences to this choice?** *More cost in the house, so more financial responsibility, more maintenance and upkeep.*

**What is the main reason you want this?** *To have more space for my family so we can thrive.*

From these questions, information is consciously gathered about what you are wanting to make a decision for; and therefore you have your why. In asking the above questions you are gathering information to help you consciously set an intention, you are identifying what you want from your intention, and are gathering potential insights as to what the outcome may be, on both the pro and con sides. If you ever doubt the choice you make, you will have the answers to these questions reminding you why you made the choice in the first place, by either remembering your answers or going through the questions again to discover if this is still what you want. Analyzing the potential pros and cons will prepare you for potential consequences of your choice, and at the same time remind you there are consequences to choice-making (good and bad). You can at any time reassess a choice and see if it is still delivering what you want.

What you want might shift over time. There might be new information around this choice that pops up, different from the pros and cons you had previously considered, that may propel you to make a different choice, or change your mind altogether. For example, you might get the big house and the kids never want to step foot outside, or there is forest fire smoke all summer and they cannot safely play outside. When these changes happen and something you want does not turn out the way you expected, realize a part of life is not really knowing outcomes, as things do not always turn out the way you want. *Reality check*. When things do not turn out as expected, it is beneficial to go back to the basis of your choice. What was the main reason you chose this for? And continue on with a reality check.

A reality check includes adding truth to a situation. Truths are facts such as what you are doing something for (or your why), as that is one of your personal truths. Truths also include things that happen as part of being human, or to the earth, or in the universe. Understanding that events sometimes happen in life that interfere with how we want our life to be is a part of the human experience. This is a reality check. Forest fires happen and destroy the air quality.

*Reality check.* If you cannot live with this you can choose to move, or wait it out as not every summer will have a fire. In the example of your children not wanting to play outside. Some children are more apt to stay in. *Reality check.* There are also video games and other technology that capture our children's focus in a way that can keep them glued to the screen and not desire other activities. *Reality check.* To support you through your children not wanting to play outside, you can find out what their wants are, and what their intentions are about staying in by asking questions, and maybe you will find information that will support you to encourage them going out. For example you might find out your children are scared of wasps and they want to stay in because there is a wasp nest in the back yard. Them being scared of wasps is one of your children's truth in this example.

Doing reality checks and asking questions to help you find truths is part of the assertive process. Often times we sit back and think how we want things to be or we wonder why someone is not doing what we want, and we never ask the questions that could provide us the information. For example, maybe your child is playing too many video games and you can say, "It is important to me that you play outside. I bought this house with a large yard so you can play safely. What is an outside game you like to play?" Asking questions about what it is you are doing something for, expressing what you want, and asking other people questions to learn more about their intentions, are all assertive skills. In the assertive skills section in the book you will gain many tools on how to ask these types of questions. Assertiveness will support you in your family relationships; in all your relationships; and in attaining what you want.

## Remember What You Wanted Something For

The exercise in the previous section was to help you determine your "What For" or your "Why" you chose something. Oftentimes too when people get what they want it does not look like they thought it would. This discrepancy can cause people to not appreciate what they have. When people discover that the situation or item they attained does not look exactly like they thought it should people become disappointed and turn away from what they wanted and begin to only focus on the parts of the situation or item that they did not want, or did not expect. When you find yourself seeing that what you wanted does not look like you think it should, instead of throwing away what you actually wanted, this is the time to reassess and remember what you made the decision to attain the situation or item for. Utilize reality checks around the decision, and discover if it is what you wanted, remember why you wanted it, and discover if what you want has changed. What parts work for you? What could be different? Sometimes just sitting down and asking these questions is enough to switch your brain from your expectations and realize that you actually have what you wanted.

I have used the remembering what I wanted something for exercise with a job. I wanted a job being a manager with a staff under me, with travel, and a good salary. When it manifested, I was a first ecstatic and hopeful, then as time went on I realized the time it took from my personal life. My job was taking up many hours of my life. I said, "I do not want my job to take over my life!" and I sat in self-pity. In the past I might have quit my job at this point. However, from an assertive and emotionally wise stand point from my training, I chose to look at my job from a different perspective. I asked myself, "What is it in my job that I do want?" I wanted the responsibility, I wanted the staff, I wanted to travel, I wanted the salary, determining I had everything I wanted. I did not foresee that to get these things at this job it meant I spent a lot more time at work and would be less available for my family.

So I asked, "What do I want now, based on this information?" I decided I wanted to spend less time working and I wanted to develop a healthier work life balance. Based on this reflection, my new conscious choices became: I will stay in my job and delegate more work to other people to help with the workload, and I will work toward developing the work-life balance I want and see if it is possible to obtain by ensuring I take time for lunch, take scheduled breaks, and only work afterhours if there is a real emergency. I also decided during this process, if another job offers the same type of responsibilities with more pay, and healthier work-life balance, I would consider a change. I also added, if after six months of actively employing the changes to support a healthier work life balance, and my work-life balance has not changed, I will actively seek different options. This entire plan above illustrates me finding out there was an element in what I wanted that was not working for me (an unbalanced work-life) and me choosing to move towards what I wanted (attaining a healthy work life balance in a situation that also had all the elements I wanted in a job). I gave myself a suitable timeline to attain the changes I actively and consciously wanted to make, and seeing if changing my actions made a difference. At any time during the six months I could re-assess, give a new time line, or try other methods. For me during the past the six months my work-life balance improved, and I decided to continue with the job and appreciate it. Sometimes a job is just too much, and sometimes it is something you can change. Trying your best with methodologies and mindsets that support you will let you know if what you are doing is what you want, or if the situation or items are just not working out for you.

## *Consequences of Emotions and Choices*

There are consequences to everything we do. Accepting a new job, not accepting a job, going into a relationship, choosing to end a relationship, having children, not having children. We cannot not know the outcome, and we live with our choices. However, knowing how emotions work, how the different parts of our psyche operate together, and how the subconscious actively seeks information from our past to try and help us make choices are golden nuggets that can support us in making more conscious choices. Even with conscious choices we do not know the outcomes. Even if it is proven time and time again that driving into water will sink our car, there are miracles and oddities that can occur to change things, such as driving into water and really the lake is shallower than we knew, and we end up driving safely across. Or, the opposite, driving a boat down a river that is normally easy to pass, and the water is shallower than expected, and the boat bottoms out and becomes stuck.

We only know information from what has happened, and what is happening now. We reach into the future with hope, and try to make things happen for us based on logical reasoning. However there are finite details that we do not know about the past, present, and future, and we cannot know everything. Being human requires courage, even more so because of the emotions we feel and our displays of courage to move forward despite past results.

# PART III

## COMMUNICATION CHOICES

# CHAPTER 9

## FOUR COMMUNICATION STYLE CHOICES

Assertiveness is one of four communication style choices which include: passive, passive aggressive, aggressive, and assertive. Communication is more than words. Communication includes our body language, our tones, our sighs, how fast we speak, as well as the words we choose. Below are descriptions and examples of each of the four communication choices that will support your assertiveness practice. Each one of these communication styles have their own patterns that develop when used often, and each style can potentially become an automatic response in different situations.

Some people are more apt to choose passive, whereas some people are more apt to choose aggressive responses. Sometimes people choose passive responses in some situations, and in other situations choose to be aggressive. Assertive communication is not often taught. We develop patterns of communication often unconsciously by either copying the patterns of our families or developing our own program of communication patterns in response to the patterns of our family and situations we experience. We repeat what has worked for us to attain what we want. For example if a person is brought up in an aggressive household, that persons will likely end up developing an aggressive or passive aggressive communication style pattern (copying of the pattern), or developing a passive communication style (an alternate response pattern). When you are aware of the four communication styles, you will become more aware of the choices you are making by patterns, or also known as habits or programs.[4] Once you are aware of what your automatic default patterns are in different situations, you can shift into using assertive skills to help assertive responses be your new pattern.

## *Passive*

Passive communication is putting the needs of others before yourself. It is not stating clearly what you want. It is valuing the opinion of others over your own self opinion. Passivity is letting others tell you what to think. It is cooping up all the thoughts about what you really feel, and really want to say and experience, but not speaking or sharing your thoughts aloud. Being passive is when you hear something that bothers you and you do not say something. Someone tells you how you feel, even though you do not feel that way, and you do not correct them. People call you by the wrong name and you do not correct them. It is letting others say and do onto you without you communicating with them

---

[4]  In neural-linguistic programming (NLP), when you respond in the same way to a similar situation, these patterns are referred to as programs, as the repeated behaviour is imprinted in the brain by repeated synapses similar to how a computer runs the same circuits to respond to a command.

what you want, what your needs are, or what you like or do not like. Passivity is also not making eye contact (in North American culture), not speaking up, or not speaking loud enough for others to hear.

Passivity is bottling up your truth and bottling up truth takes energy. This energy builds up mentally, emotionally, and physically within your body and mind. Some people become so good at bottling their true feelings and thoughts, it becomes easy and they do not feel the pressure of keeping things in. As they grow accustomed to the pressure as being their normal, they go on living quite comfortably in this passivity. The pressure of keeping true feelings and thoughts tamped down and from leaking out steals energy. Choosing passivity can work for you and be comfortable when you have trusting people around you who do not cross your unspoken boundaries, who are kind, and who value you.

Passivity is one of the communication choices I am very familiar with. I spent most of my childhood and youth not loving myself and "going with the flow", yet in not such a carefree way. I followed others and fell into crowds of people who would "like" me. By following others and devaluing my own opinions, I did not learn things or do things that I truly liked. I listened to music others liked, watched television shows others liked, and chose activities others liked. I did not like myself. I did not speak my mind. If I did speak my mind and someone did not agree, I physically felt injured in my solar plexus and my throat, and would quickly change my opinion to theirs. I would ruminate about not being liked, or something I had said, for days, until I could find solace or until I could replace those feelings by being liked by, or being agreed with by, someone else.

Passivity is seen as good guy behaviour, or rather good girl behaviour. Passivity is "not rocking the boat" and it also is going along with persons or rules of the authority when you do not agree with what the authority is asking you to do. For centuries it was actually expected that women be passive and if a woman spoke out or "acted out" she was considered neurotic, or her husband was told to shut her up and deal with her. Things have changed in society where women have more of a voice, however a lot of women still default to passive communication. This is due to the communication patterns we have learned from the women in our life and from society. Women also pass these communication patterns down to their daughters, nieces, and granddaughters. When people are passive they are seen as agreeable and easy to get along with, because they do not challenge another person's point of view or action. People chose passivity because it is more likely they will be liked. Men are less often expected to be passive, especially in their communication towards women. When men act passively they can be made fun of or thought to be less successful, or less manly, by others. Men learn from an early age that the more passive you are, the less successful you will be, and therefore choose a different communication style. Or if they continue in passive communication, they might have a negative concept of themselves and self-esteem.

## Consequences to Passivity

There are consequences to each communication choice we make. Consequences of passive communication are feeling walked on continuously but keeping all the feelings inside, feeling unable to speak up, low self-esteem, and developing an inner rage. Putting others continuously first means not taking care of yourself, therefore it is possible to become ill more often, be more tired, and be more stressed. Being passive does not normally get you what you want. Sometimes it can support you if you are dealing with a person who is acting aggressively when you can intentionally act passive to appease that person to give you enough time to figure out how to exit the situation. Overall, continually being passive by not expressing yourself and keeping in your true feelings builds up internal pressure where you either suffer in silence, or eventually ends up exploding into aggression or passive aggression.

## *Passive Aggressive*

Passive aggressive communication is similar to passive communication where a person chooses to not speak her or his mind, yet chooses at the same time to take an aggressive action. An example of passive aggressive communication is slamming dishes around when you are mad that no one is helping you, yet at the same time not asking for help. Or you have asked for help with the dishes and your teens are sitting on the couch playing video games and they have refused to help, or said, "Later." Instead of expressing you want them to help and you want it done now, you choose instead to slam cupboards to express your dissatisfaction. When someone asks in response to your dish slamming, "Are you ok?" a passive aggressive response would be "I am fine" in a harsh sharp tone, or a higher pitched tone.

I once used some special oil to cook with that belonged to a family member and she was very mad at me, but I did not know she was mad until later. One day I was going through one of my drawers and something very special to me was missing. I asked her if she knew where the item went. She told me she threw it out. I asked why. She told me because I used her cooking oil. The family member had taken the item from my drawer as revenge for me using her cooking oil by taking and disposing of something I cared about. If I had not asked her about the missing item, I never would have known I upset her. By asking her why she threw out my special item, I was choosing assertive communication, and her truthful response was also assertive. If she had continued using passive aggressive communication in response to my questioning, instead of telling me why, she would have either lied to me or would not have answered my question directly such as stating something such as, "Where do you think it went?" in a patronizing tone, or by not answering my question at all and instead stopping out of the room in response.

Passive aggressive communication is also stealing office supplies or toilet paper from work thinking, "They owe me," or, "I didn't get the raise so..." which are not often conscious thoughts, but are usually hidden intentions behind the action of stealing the supplies. Other examples of passive aggressive communication are: stomping your feet walking away from a conflict; lying to hide the truth; using patronizing tones and reflecting questions back onto others in the spirit that you think they should know what you are thinking; and giving the silent treatment.

## Consequences to Passive Aggressive

It does not feel good for either party when a person is choosing passive aggressive communication. It hurts the person choosing passive aggression in a similar way to when someone chooses passivity. The pent up unspoken true thoughts and feelings have built up causing great discomfort, and the actions taken in passive aggression such as slamming cupboards, are an outlet of that discomfort. The aggressive actions in passive aggression are unconstructive actions that often place all parties involved in an awkward position. There is normally a lot of tension inside the person acting passive aggressively, and the action taken is a way to release the tension, yet the words chosen do not match the action.

Other people can feel that tension, whether or not they are conscious of it, and there is an underlying sense that something is not right for both parties. Passive aggressive communication hurts others because the actions taken when acting passive aggressively are quite intense. The actions in passive aggressive communication do not match the words used, or if any words are used they normally sends conflicting messages. The contrasting actions and words send a conflicting message and this is unsettling to people. For example, the conflicting message of stating "I am fine" in an escalated sharp tone while slamming the kitchen cupboards communicates that person is not telling the truth. That person is not fine, that person is slamming the cupboards. People around the person acting passive aggressively stops trusting that person, or sometimes stop trusting themselves, as the mixed messages show that person is not being truthful or if the person is being truthful the person witnessing the passive aggression might question their perception. Either of these examples of response makes bystanders to the behaviour feel uneasy. Another consequence of passive aggressive communication could be that you still do not get what you want, or if you do, you get it in a way that hurts someone else. Passive aggression hurts others because it is confusing and is paired with an intense emotion that the person is trying very hard to contain. That pent up emotion and tension leak out in unsettling behaviours that affect all involved.

## When Passive Aggression Becomes Abuse

Passive aggression can also become abuse. When a person speaks one way with their body and not with their words, it hurts people. I have been in a relationship where a man giving me the silent treatment made the atmosphere in the room feel heavy. I had to step on eggshells to not upset him. During the silent treatment he refused to look at me or talk to me. It made me feel sick to my stomach. I cared for him and wanted to help. He obviously felt hurt, but instead of sharing what hurt him, he played a game to make me feel hurt, and I did not know why. This is very harmful and hurtful to a caring loving partner because a caring loving person wants to care for and work things out in a relationship. If you are in a relationship with someone who does this, your best response is to let them know you care about them and want to work this out. Tell them when they are ready to work it out to let you know, and then you go do something for you. You cannot control the person's actions. Realize they are not acting in a healthy manner. Instead of playing their game, step away from the situation and focus on something you want to do instead. Separate yourself from the energy. Trust that because you communicated to them when they are ready to talk through it you will be there, they will eventually be ready to talk through it. When they are ready to discuss what they feel, then real repair can happen for both people. I am sure almost every one of us has used the silent treatment, however the silent treatment can be abusive if used intentionally to hurt another person.

Imagine what happens when the silent treatment is used with children. Children are big energy sponges and the adult who is supposed to love them is bottling up all the anger and frustration and refuses to acknowledge the child. Children will feel the energy of the tension, know something is wrong, and will think it is their fault as they will think they are causing the emotion and tension in the other person. Children are intelligent, intuitive, and emotionally connected beings who are also completely innocent loving beings learning reality through their role models. If the child asks what is wrong and the silent treatment continues, they will default to thinking they did something wrong or something is wrong with them as their (and all of our) subconscious looks for an answer. To a child their world is normally made up of their caregiver and themselves. If the caregiver says nothing is wrong or will not satisfy the child's inquiry, the next best answer in a child's perspective is something must be wrong with the child that caused the caregiver to not love him or her anymore or caused the caregiver not to acknowledge him or her. It hurts children deeply when adults and caregivers choose to use the silent treatment. Children take on the responsibility of the person giving the silent treatment, take on that persons emotions, and take the blame for that persons actions.

When cupboards are slammed around kids, they learn to take their aggression out on objects instead of talking through issues, feelings, and uncomfortable thoughts with words. When a child senses something is wrong while witnessing aggressive actions and the person displaying those actions says, "Nothing is wrong," The child learns to not trust their intuition. If nothing is wrong with the person who is being passive aggressive (because they were told by that person nothing is wrong) then the child concludes that something must be wrong with themselves, because that is the next possibility.

It is very important how we act as people when we are role models for children. And it is not always our fault, as we can be perfect parents (um... okay not perfect, let us say close to perfect parents), and our kids will still grow up to be their own person, which may or may not include positive actions or choices. It is important to consider how we are acting and what we are teaching as parents, caregivers, uncles, aunts, or grandparents, because our children look up to us and learn from us what is appropriate and acceptable behaviour. Children will accept as crossable, the boundaries that we cross. If we give silent treatments, children will learn to give silent treatments. If our children use a silent treatment, we need to teach them it is not appropriate and a more resourceful constructive choice is to talk through their thoughts and feelings to express what is going on for them. The silent treatment is a form of power over another person as the person is not acknowledging you or reacting/responding to you, and it is used by a person when that person feels they have no power. Sometimes when a person, an adult or a child, feels powerless, the silent treatment or other passive aggressive actions are an act of power. However, passive aggression harbours feelings that are not dealt with and build up. If passive aggression is used often or is encouraged by results, using passive aggressive communication becomes a pattern and a go-to solution for situations. This forms an unhealthy communication pattern for the person and the people around that person.

## *Aggressive*

Aggression consists of yelling, kicking, screaming, rushing others unnecessarily, pointing forcefully, calling names, gossipping, hitting, demanding rather than asking, and is physical and or verbal violence. People who choose aggression, like any of the communication styles, do so because it has worked for them to get their way, and like any of the four styles of communication, there are consequences.

Oftentimes we feel justified when we use aggression. I lashed out at my husband's ex-wife one evening. The evening I lashed out I arrived home after picking up a prescription for my son who had an ear infection and I myself had a fever and the flu. She was parked in front of our house blocking our driveway, and was loading my daughter's bike into her van. No one had told me she was coming to our house nor did I give any permission for her to have my daughter's bike. At first I was assertive. I rolled down my window and asked in an inquisitive tone, "What are you doing?" She responded, "Oh, Frank said I could have this bike for Debbie."[5] I remained assertive when I responded, " That is my daughter's bike, I would like the chance to ask her if she wants it any longer first before we give it away." She responded in a sharp snotty tone, "Well Frank said I could have it." I, beginning to lose my cool and my tone becoming harsh (and my emotions were growing), repeated, "It is my daughter's bike. I want to ask her first." She responded passive aggressively. She turned away from me and looked directly at Frank and stated to him sharply, "Just give her back the damn bike." At that point I lost it. In my mind she was blocking my driveway preventing me from going home and getting my son his prescription, she was taking my daughter's bike, and she just completely dismissed me on my property while taking my property. I held a lot of anger toward her from some of the actions that she had taken around Frank's relationship with his and her children during the past few years. I blew up and yelled, "I am tired of everything. I have only been nice to you when you speak so poorly of Frank. You speak badly about him in front of his children. I am tired of this and I will not take it anymore, get off my property." I was yelling, and pointing at her. For a moment I even got out of my car. I realized as soon as I got out of my car how bad this was escalating. I got back in my car and toned it down a bit. The worst thing is Frank's daughter was there and she came out to defend her mom. I told her that I love her and she was welcome anytime but her mom had to get off my property. It was not a moment to be proud of.

The consequences of this were that she would not allow Frank's five year old to come over anymore for sleep overs

---

[5]   Names changed for anonymity

because she said I was not a stable person. Although this angered me and I saw this as a story spun for her to isolate Frank's children from him further, my actions were not okay either. Her rule was before she would let their son visit, I had to apologize first. I was mad at Frank also as he sat back and watched the whole situation and he did not stand up for me or support me. I was ultimately standing up for him because the real reason behind my anger was many of her actions before this moment. I had finally expressed how I truly felt aloud, and it seemed like he took her side. It was not until almost one year after the event that my husband informed me how important it was to him that I apologized for this. I apologized to the woman but framed it as I am sorry I yelled in front of her daughter, as that was the biggest part of the mistake, and was something I agreed I did wrong. If either Frank or I were assertive with each other and discussed this situation and how it affected each of us, I might have known earlier about how important it was to him that I apologize. I thought he did not support me and this affected how I saw and felt about our relationship. We could have talked about my feelings as well and cleared up any doubts about this and added value to our relationship.

What could I have done differently? I could have said, "No, you are not taking the bike until my daughter can have a say in this," and no matter what her response, hold my ground. When she turned to dismiss me, ignoring my request and instead responded to Frank, I could have seen this as a passive aggressive act, knowing it for what it was, take a few extra deep breaths, and not let her actions get to me. If I took a moment to stop, breathe, and do a reality check, I would have noticed her daughter was there. If I noticed her daughter was there, I would have realized this was not the time to express my anger because I love his daughter and did not want to hurt her. Since I had an issue with her talking bad about Frank to his kids, I could have scheduled a meeting with her with a mediator to discuss my concerns. I could have also said, "I have a fever and am not feeling well. You are blocking the driveway. I need to get into my home and give my son antibiotics. Please move your van, and please do not take the bike today until I can ask my daughter." Her behaviour was also not healthy or assertive in this situation, yet it did not give me an excuse to treat her the way I did. It made me the "bad guy" even though it was not my normal behaviour. Using aggression can end up having larger consequences that last a lifetime.

## Consequences to Aggression

Aggression is seen as the most unhealthy communication style as it can hurt your family members, friends, colleagues, and can land you in jail. Aggression is what our children use when they feel they have no power. Adults are bigger than children and adults make all the rules. Children have not yet developed a set of skills about how to respectfully attain what they want or how to express their own power and place in the world. Adult people who use aggression are not much different than a child using aggression as they also feel they have no power in the situation, and escalate their body language, their word use, their tones, and speed of speech to get what they want. Aggression hurts the person being aggressive and hurts all those involved. Everyone loses. The person using aggression is seen as unsafe or unstable. Their target normally ends up feeling belittled, insulted, or injured.

Using aggression does not mean you are a bad person. It means that this is what has worked for you, at the expense of others, and at the expense of yourself. It also means there might be a part of you that is hurting or feeling powerless. Aggression is a form of lashing out similar to how a cornered injured animal might lash out. One way of changing behaviour is learning more about the emotion behind your communication choices and behind how you choose to treat people. Another way to change your behaviour is being aware when you choose certain communication styles, and when a situation comes up you normally would be aggressive in, you can choose to try something different. Even after an aggressive bout of behaviour, you can always stop yourself, re-establish control of your choices, and profess, "What I just said was aggressive. What I am trying to say is...." and restate what you are wanting to say in an assertive manner.

## *When Aggression Becomes Abuse*

Aggression can turn into abuse if it escalates or is used very often. If you have hit or physically or verbally hurt someone, you cannot take that back. You can own up to it, and apologize, however at this point it has gone too far and it destroys relationships. Calling names, verbally or physically hurting others affects people on a deep level. Acting verbally and physically violent is a choice. If this is something you do, ask yourself questions such as, "What about this behaviour supports me? What about this is good for my family? How does this align with who I want to be?" and find a good life coach to work with you through this. People are not born abusive. Like most behaviours, people learn abusive behaviours from people around them or as behaviours are exercised. People will keep using abusive behaviours when the results they want are gained from using the behaviours. People also continue to use abusive behaviours when they believe or feel they have no other choices, possibly because nothing else has worked for them, or when other behaviours utilized did not work as quickly.

One of the main reasons I am writing this book is to offer information so people can make different choices, and to help people get more of what they want in a way that is respectful to others. The information is also offered to support building stronger relationships.

When you have chosen a pattern of abuse, you cannot make what you have done better. You cannot take away your past actions. However, you can take responsibility for your behaviours and acknowledge how it is wrong to treat people that way. Accept your past and choose differently in the future. No amends will fix the hurt caused in the past, and you may never be forgiven for it. It is a tough road yet you as a person can change your behaviour and self-identity at any moment. You can always make a different choice the next time. The sooner you choose a different communication style that is more respectful, the sooner you will treat people better and stop unhealthy or hurtful patterns. It is never too late to stop a pattern. On the other hand, consequences of past behaviours are something we all have to live with. *Reality check.*

## *Aggression as the Bad Guy Behaviour*

Although I have gone heavily into aggression in this section of the book, and have painted it as the "bad guy" behaviour, it is needed in life. In situations when we are being attacked or when our kids are being hurt, aggression might be required. We have access to, and have biological tendencies towards aggression as the fight part of the fight or flight behaviour, and sometimes we need to fight. When it is our safety or our children's safety, aggression is required. Each communication style has its moment of use, and each exists for a reason. People use what works for them, and people also have used all four of these communication styles at some point in their life. Often times we see situations as threatening when they are not, like my husband's ex-wife blocking the driveway and taking my daughters bike, like an executive thinking his assistant is challenging his point of view, like the parent who hits the child because they did not listen to him; these are all examples of misused aggression.

## *Assertive*

Assertiveness is speaking up from yourself in a way that is respectful to yourself and others. It is knowing how to say no. It is valuing your position and the positions of others while still standing strong in yourself, and noticing how others stand in their selves. It is recognizing how the psyche works; how we non-consciously act from past behaviours, beliefs, and values, and recognizing that others do the same; it is recognizing where others are coming from so we can respond wisely; and it is recognizing where we are coming from so we can shift and move into how we truly want to act instead of reacting unconsciously. Assertiveness is standing tall, is having a voice, is speaking even when we are scared, is having emotional wisdom where we understand how emotions work, and knowing how to move forward and through our emotions in a way that supports us. Assertiveness lifts people out of depressions; it reduces stress; it increases relationship and job satisfaction; it is acceptance of situations; it improves decision-making skills; it is a lighthouse in the dark; it is courage; it builds self-esteem; and it builds strong people who exercise power with others versus power over others. Assertive communication is also a learned skill. By using assertiveness you have a better chance at getting what you want and also increasing your overall well-being.

Assertive communication is the most respectful style of communication for yourself and for others and often gives you rewarding results. It is the best way to ask for what you want, share what you feel or think, or add your point of view and expertise. Like the other communication styles, there are also consequences to using assertive communication.

## Consequences to Assertive Communication

Some people might find your assertiveness off-putting especially when they are used to people responding passively to them and in response they might respond aggressively. Or, a person might respond passively to assertive communication if they are not used to other people speaking their point of view clearly and asking for what they want, as it can be seen as intimidating. If you are a woman and you are speaking up or standing up for yourself in a group, it can be seen as "bitchy." Sometimes a man in a group of more dominating men might be made fun of when finally speaking up. No matter the dynamics of a situation, it is okay to speak up because you are speaking from yourself, from your truth, and when done so assertively you are speaking in a respectful way toward others, and you know where you are coming from. You cannot control the reaction of others. You can use skills and tools to help you navigate the reactions other people have which are offered to you in Part IV of this book. Of note, even when using assertive techniques, if people around you are not used to you speaking up, it can be off-putting at first. As you practice and assert yourself more often, the people around you will get used to you being assertive, and benefit from you being assertive. The assertive stance is a stance of respect, is sharing information from your true self, and communicating in the best way possible.

## *Summary of Communication Style Choices*

You can choose any of the four communication styles at any time. People are not one of these communication choices, yet people often define themselves and others as being passive, aggressive, passive aggressive, or assertive. No matter how a person is defined, they are still free to choose to act differently. People who define themselves as passive can easily act aggressively. For example when people have been taken advantage of, or walked on for a long time, they can easily lash out. After the lash out they may become shattered and question if they even know themselves any longer. The truth is passivity, aggression, passive aggression, and assertiveness are not fixed aspects of a person. These are communication choices. When a choice works out for you over and over again, it is more likely the choice you will choose next time. At any time you can choose differently. A person who normally chooses passive can choose aggression. A person who normally chooses aggression can choose assertive. There is enough information in this book to support your choices. Sometimes it is wise to be passive, sometimes is it wise to be aggressive. I guarantee that when you start choosing assertiveness most often, you will see results and get more of what you want in life. Relationships have room to grow, while you grow, standing tall in the strength and respect that assertive communication and behaviour has to offer. In the next section there are multiple techniques and tools to help you build your assertive communication, responses, and practice.

# PART IV:

## ASSERTIVE COMMUNICATION TECHNIQUES

# CHAPTER 10

## COMMUNICATION TECHNIQUES

Below are assertive communication techniques described to support your assertive practice. Some techniques are physical, such as use of body language and tone, some are verbal, such as methods of speaking, words to use; and some more mental, such as using empathy. Each of these techniques work in tandem and can be mixed. There are times one of these techniques will work better than others.

### *Body Language*

Body language is a very important part to all of our communication and oftentimes speaks louder than words. Assertive body language is generally standing tall, arms uncrossed, making eye contact, and pairing this with using appropriate tone for the situation. Using your body language to support your communication also requires reading the situation. For example, when someone is feeling unheard you can lean in toward them to show you are listening, nodding your head often. If someone is being overpowering, it helps if you ensure you are on their level. If they are standing up you stand up to display your equality. Put your hands on your hips or place your hands down and out at your sides with your arms open slightly from your body to make yourself look bigger. If you are shaking, placing your hands at your hips or folding your hands in front of you can help reduce the shaking. Trust me, not many people will notice you shaking anyway as they are more focused on themselves than on you. Assertive body language when you are sitting includes keeping both feet on the floor and ensuring your shoulders are back, sitting tall. Many leadership teachers have their students perform the superman (or superwoman) pose before a meeting or giving a speech. This pose is when you stand with your hands at your hips and push your chest out, acting like you are wearing a cape. This position helps you feel powerful and supports courage. The simple change of keeping your shoulders back and sitting up straight supported one of the people in my courses immensely, and is an easy change you can start making now.

If you notice yourself shaking while learning to express yourself, please know that the shaking will go away with practice. It is a natural thing to go through while we reach beyond our usual comfort levels. I was trained to speak in front of groups during my social work education. For the first six months of me doing presentations, my voice shook, and so did most of my body. After practicing and continuing to show up to do the presentations, the shaking just went away. I did not even notice when it changed, it just stopped. Most people do not even notice you are shaking anyway as most people are focused on their own thoughts and feelings most of the time. Those that do notice you shaking will likely be compassionate and think how strong you are for speaking up anyway. I will let you in on a little secret, I do still shake at times when I give presentations. It depends on where I am at on that day mentally, physically, emotionally, and how often I have been practicing. I have learned to show up anyway and I remind myself that speaking in front of others is a skill and just by doing it, I am doing something courageous.

If you come across people who notice and choose to belittle you for shaking, use this observation as information, and remember their belittling actually is not about you but is about something inside of them. People who belittle, feel little inside, and see you as stronger, or feel the need to be stronger than you. If someone in your life is belittling you, it gives you an opportunity to decide if you want to be around that person. We go further into this throughout the book because although people who belittle are harmful, there is a lot more behind their behaviour, and assertiveness training can support them as well. If you are a person who chooses to belittle others, please keep reading. Assertiveness practice and training supports building a true self esteem from which you can operate and be connected to your true self, instead of operating from the self you have created to mask underlying beliefs about yourself that most likely were handed down from someone else or that you had to create to feel okay.

## Tone and Speed of Speech

Tone is an integral part of assertive communication. Different tones are required in different situations, and when emotions are running high, keeping an appropriate tone for the situation might be challenging. Keeping a calm even voice is the best in most situations and supports assertive communication. How fast you speak also is part of communication. When you speak rapidly, others will have a harder time following what you are saying, or you may come across as nervous. Also think about your breathing. When you speak very quickly it is harder to catch your breath. If you speak in a calm even tone it is easier to breathe, and calm breathing promotes a calm respectful demeaner. If you speak very slowly, people may stop listening, or have a hard time focusing on what you are saying, because they are waiting for their turn to talk and are thinking all the things they want to say.

When someone is approaching you in a way you think is unsafe become louder and yell, "YOU IN THE GREEN SHIRT, DO NOT COME NEAR ME!" Notice how the statement called out something he or she is wearing. This is intentional so that person realizes they are able to be described. People with intention harm normally do not like to be identifiable, because if you can identify what they look like, you can describe them accurately to the police, and they will more likely be caught. Yelling and being very loud is appropriate when you are being targeted or attacked. In most situations speaking clearly and calmly is appropriate. As you practice assertive communication you might start out speaking and your voice comes out shaky, or maybe you are normally very quiet and when you start using assertive communication you end up speaking in a soft voice, or maybe you end up speak in a harsh tone as you practice. All three of these are normal growing pains of learning to use assertiveness. Each new situation in which you try using assertiveness is an opportunity to ask yourself what worked, and what did not work. And lucky enough, life will give you multiple opportunities to practice assertiveness. It is called an assertive practice because it is a continual path of growth and discovery, and adjustments are required to respond to life's experiences, as you build a way to consciously show up in the world assertively. Learn to work with yourself as you develop your assertive practice and reflect on experiences, "Okay, so the last time I was a bit harsh toned trying to speak my mind, now let me try to soften my voice a little and see what happens." Or, "The last time I used too soft a tone, the person could not really hear me, and I did not come across confident in what I was saying. Let me try a little louder next time."

## *Using "I" statements*

Using "I" statements is one of the easiest changes you can make towards communicating more assertively. Look at the difference:

*"I think there is a better way of dealing with this than yelling at the kids, such as giving them a time out."*
(Stating a point of view)
**Versus**
*"You yelling at the kids is not appropriate."* (Blaming)

*"I feel hurt when you yell at me and I don't like it."*
(Stating how you feel and your position)
**Versus**
*"You hurt me when you yell at me."*
(Blaming; giving the responsibility to someone else for how you feel)

In the example above, you are the one choosing to feel hurt, even though feeling hurt is a natural reaction to being yelled at. The other person cannot choose how you feel, although yes sometimes people yell to make you feel bad on purpose. Many times people yell because they feel they do not have any other power or option in the situation. Using "I" statements separates you from the other person, which is setting a boundary. When using "I" statements you are showing understanding that you and the other person are two separate beings and your interpretation and feelings come from yourself and do not belong to the other person.

## *Changing Verbs*

Simply changing the verbs you use supports speaking more assertively. Listen to the difference:

*I could do that* **versus** *I will do that*
*I need this job* **versus** *I want this job*
*I need you to listen to me* **versus** *I want you to listen to me*
*I have to go to work today* **versus** *I choose to go to work today*
*I have to go to karate* **versus** *I choose to go to karate*

Which one sounds more confident or certain? Which one is more assertive? The words we use do communicate more than we realize. For example, "could" is a form of non-commitment and part of assertiveness is keeping your word. "I will" is agreeing you will do something, and is more certain. "Need" is less proactive than "want," as "need" comes from a place of lack (meaning you do not have something). "Want" comes from a place of moving toward a goal. "Have to" takes away from the fact you are choosing, and using the word "choosing" states you have agency and you recognize your power of choice. The words you use in other parts of your speech can affect you as well. Using words that enrich what you are communicating enrich your life and enrich your value. Words are connected to memories and neural pathways. When we change the words we use to more certain, clear, confident, and valuable words, we create more certain, clear, confident, and valuable patterns and connections in our brain.

## *Saying No*

Saying no is one of the more difficult things for some people to say and often comes up in the group work I do. People who do not like saying no either do not want to hurt someone else's feelings, or think they might miss out on something if they say no. Sometimes people are even scared to say no to authority figures or to a parent figure or family member. Saying no could be perceived as not fulfilling your duty at work or at home. However, saying no is important. If you say yes all the time you will end up agreeing to things that you do not want or like, or you could end up in dangerous situations.

Sometimes we do say yes to things we do not really want for practical reasons, such as doing the dishes or laundry. On the other hand, there are times we feel obligated to do something we do not want to do, even though it is something that does not need to be done. Maybe your Mom wants you to come over and help her clean her house on the weekend, however you have had a rough week and were looking forward to some alone time. Part of you wants to go because it is your Mom, and she will be upset you will not help, or might guilt you because you say no. It is your choice ultimately to go or to take the time for yourself. It is your priority choice. What do you prioritize? There is no wrong or right answer here. Priorities change based on how you feel and change under different circumstances. What is most valuable to you in this choice at this time? At one time cleaning your Mom's house might have higher value, and at another time taking time for yourself might. How do you say no to your Mom or to others that you care about or feel an obligation to? Below are some examples of how to say no.

## *The Rain-check No*

The rain-check no is saying no for now and scheduling a different time to do what is asked or to answer a question.

**Example:** Your Mom wants you to come help her clean her house this weekend yet you do not want to go:
*"I cannot come over this weekend Mom, however I can come over next weekend to help you clean your house."*
   **Or**
*"Mom, at this time I cannot commit to coming over to help you clean your house this weekend, I will know better on Thursday if I can help or not."*

**Example:** A friend asks you to a party, however you are not sure yet if you want to go. Using the rain-check no gives you time to answer:
*"I am saying no now, however I will know better on Tuesday if I can go to the party or not and will let you know if I change my mind."*

**Example:** Someone asks you out to coffee tomorrow but that does not work for you, and you do want to go out for coffee with this person:
*"I cannot make it Tuesday, however I would be available on Saturday."*

## *The Reasoned No*

The reasoned no is saying no and also providing a reason. The trick is to provide a brief and true reason. A true reason supports your position if the person tries to push you further, rather than you having to stumble in response to a mistruth.

**Example:** Someone asks you to go out for dinner tonight and you want to say no:

*"No thank you, I have promised my daughter I would watch movies with her tonight."*
  **Or**
*If you are not interested at all you can clearly say, "No thank you, I am not interested in going out to dinner."*

**Example:** Someone one asks you to do an extra report at work and you are swamped with other work commitments. *"No, I am unable to do the extra report you are requesting. I am working on completing my commitments for month end."*

## The Empathetic or Reflective No

The empathetic or reflective no involves considering the other person's feelings and saying no in the same encounter. In an empathetic or reflective no, state how you perceive the other person feels about the request they made of you, and add your refusal to their request at the end of the sentence.

**Example:** Someone wants to come over and talk about how bad their day was and you are not up to it.
*"I understand you have had a bad day, however I am unable to have you over tonight."*

**Example:** Someone wants to talk about a major issue about a co-worker and you do not want to get in the middle of it.

*"I see you are upset, however this is a situation I do not want to be a part of."*

Notice how in the above examples using the "I" statements is incorporated. It is important to add the "I" statements as it is your perception of how they feel and the other person might feel differently than you have perceived them to feel. By saying "I see" or "I understand" gives the other person an opening to inform you about how they are really feeling if required.

## The Direct No

The direct no is simply saying "No."

**Example:** Someone asks you, *"Do you want some cake?"* You reply, *"No thank you."*

## Broken Record

The broken record technique is repeating your request or your answer to someone by keeping what you are saying the same but saying it in different ways. People generally want to get what they want and sometimes do not take no for an answer. To respond to repeated requests even if you have already said no, the broken record is restating saying no in different ways.

For example, if the person in the direct no example did not accept your no to having the cake, you can use the broken record technique.

Someone asks, *"Do you want some cake?"*
You reply, *"No thank you."*
The person continues to press, *"Come on have a piece of cake."*
You reply, *"No."*

**Example:** Your girlfriend has asked that you go out on Friday with her, but you have a hockey game to play. She is insistent you skip the game. Here is how the broken record can work:

*"Jeremy, let's go to that party on Friday."*

*"I can't I have a hockey game Friday."*

*"Come on Jeremy, we never spend time together."*

*"I do enjoy spending time with you, and I have a hockey game Friday."*

*"Jeremy, skip the game, go with me."*

*"No, I have a hockey game that night."*

*"I won't be your girlfriend anymore if you don't go with me."*

*"I am sorry you feel that way, however I have a hockey game Friday and I am not going to the party."*

The broken record is a way to stand your ground, and giving information to the other person gives them a chance to respect your stance. The broken record can also be used when someone is trying to press you for more information and you either do not have the information or you do not want to disclose the information, such as in business disputes.

**Example:** A contractor wants to know what other contractors bid on a project, and this information is confidential.

Contractor: *"What did James's company bid?"*

You: *"I am not authorized to give that information."*

Contractor: *"Come on, I need to know so I can figure out how far off I was."*

You: *"I appreciate your business and like working with you, however I cannot give that information."*

Contractor: *"Okay, I understand."*

The broken record also works when you are requesting something, such as returning an item, or getting your children to do a chore.

**Example:** You bought a pair of pants, there is a hole in the stitching, and you want to return them.

You: *"I bought these pants two days ago. When I brought it home I noticed a hole in the stitching. I want to return the pants."*

Clerk: *"Sorry Ma'am, how do I know you didn't make the hole yourself?"*

You: *"I noticed the hole after I brought it home, I would like to return the pants."*

Clerk: *"Ok, do you have your receipt?"*

**Example:** It is your son's chore to do the dishes. The dishes have not been done in a long time and are piling up in the sink.

You: *"Chris your chore is to do the dishes, and they are piled up by the sink."*

Chris: *"I will get to them later."*

You: *"The dishes are piled up at the sink, there are only a few left in the cupboard, and it your chore to ensure they are done."*

Chris: *"Later."*

You: *"Chris it is your chore to ensure the dishes are done so others can use dishes, the dishes are piled up in the sink."*

Chris: *"Okay, fine!"*

In the above example, you might need to redefine the chore such as setting a time the dishes are to be done by each day. Communication can always be improved by redefining our agreements and making sure we are on the same page. Also, you might want to set up a consequence if the chore is not done such as if the dishes are not done by five o'clock in the evening each day the internet will be taken away. Adding consequences to a request is an example of escalation.

## *Escalation*

Escalation is when you take a larger action than what you have tried previously, or add a consequence, when someone is not responding as you have asked. This can include becoming firmer in your request, by changing your tone to a more firm tone, or by explaining what you will do next if they do not do what you have asked. Escalation also can involve approaching someone with authority for support with a situation.

You can use escalation with strangers if you do not like the behaviour they are distributing towards you. For example a strange man has started approaching you and calling out to you using negative names. You yell out, "You in the green shirt, stop walking toward me or I will call the police." Calling the police is the escalation.

Escalation is also going to a manager or a person above your manager, or Human Resources for support if someone acts inappropriately towards you at work when you have asked them to stop and they continue the behaviour. For example, your boss is constantly belittling you and you have pointed out the behaviour and he makes fun of you for being sensitive. You decide to go to Human Resources and ask what else can be done and follow the directions they give you. If you do not have Human Resources you can go to a higher up manager, owner, union, or a labour board for support.

Another example, an employee was late even after you set up a development plan which included them being on time every day, and she did not have a valid reason for being late. Escalation would be to sending her a warning letter or other consequence as determined by the development plan.

Escalation can also be used with your children. For example, "If you do not stop screaming at me, I will give you a time out." Or, with older children, "If you do not do the chores I asked you to do by the time I get home, the internet is off for the rest of the day."

With escalation it is important to follow through with what you say you will do, or it will not work the next time you use this method. Also by doing what you say you are going to do, and repeating the use of escalation, for example with your children, it will show them that you mean what you say and you follow through with the consequences. In response, they will begin to learn that it is better to listen to you, because if they do not listen, they will face the consequences you have set. This is also true for adults. Adults are also continually learning and will start listening more as well if consequences stated are employed. However, an adult might also choose to move on instead of listening depending on the situation. Sometimes an adult person has not been given consequences or examples of healthy boundaries in their life. Following through on the consequences you state is an important aspect to the effectiveness of using the tool of escalation, no matter what the age of the person.

## *Ask for More Time*

Assertiveness is also being aware of where you are in a situation. Sometimes the best thing to do is ask for more time. Sometimes you are not mentally or emotionally prepared for a conversation, or you might not have an answer yet. If someone has just confronted you with something you are not prepared for such as, "Susan I am really upset with you and I want an answer now!" an assertive response would be, "I see you want an answer. However, I am not prepared for this conversation right now. I am going to take some time to gather my thoughts." If the person continues with, "No, I want an answer now!" you can respond with, "I want more time to answer you and I am leaving this conversation. I will connect with you on Tuesday," and walk away. This example also displays using the broken record technique.

## *Empathy*

When I say the word empathy what comes to mind? Empathy is often thought as feeling sorry for someone else, or being compassionate. Empathy is considering where someone else is coming from. It is stepping into someone else's shoes for a moment. It is a skill that can support you in knowing how to deliver what you want to say. Utilizing empathy is a core element in assertive communication as it considers where others are coming from, while also considering where you are coming from. Assertiveness is speaking up from yourself in a way that respects the feelings, thoughts, and values of others, while also respecting your own feelings, thoughts, and values. Assertiveness is mutual respect, respecting yourself while also respecting the other person. Empathy is a method of understanding another person's position and helps you to decide how best to respectfully respond in a situation.

For example, you might want to have a difficult conversation with someone, maybe a spouse or a friend. Using empathy would be considering the other person's possible thoughts and feelings about what you are going to say or might be saying. If you realize a conversation is going to upset someone, it does not mean you do not have the conversation. Using empathy might be deciding the right time to have the conversation, choosing the tone you deliver the information, and choosing the words you use.

I had a friend who would often come over without calling first. She would just drop by and many times usually late in the evening when I was pretty tired, but I would just invite her in. Despite being exhausted, I would have tea with her for hours, and this was unfair to me as I truly did not want the company but I was too "polite" to say how I felt. The consequence of not telling her how I felt was that I did not enjoy the company, and I did not really listen to her. After realizing how these surprise and frequent visits were affecting me, I decided to prepare for a difficult conversation. How do I tell my friend I find she comes over too much without calling me first, and I do not want that many visits? I love her and I do not want to hurt her. However, these visits do end up affecting me negatively. Reflecting on how to say this included me thinking of how it could affect my friend.

1. She may not have even realized how I felt and be instantly apologetic.
2. She might feel that I do not cherish her, or she is being unwanted.
3. She might take offense and think she did something wrong.

In this particular instance it was most possible that she would feel unwanted so I knew I needed to communicate how important she was to me. She thrives from her friendships and social life. She is an extrovert, meaning she receives energy from being with others, where as I am an introvert and I become exhausted from being in social situations for long periods of time. So I chose to deliver this conversation as follows:

*"Deborah, you are very important to me. Lately there have been many times you come over without calling first, and because*

*I cherish you I do not tell you that really I am not up for company at the time. I do love our time together and I would appreciate if moving forward you could call me first before coming over, to see if it is a good time for me also."*

This example respects both of our positions. We are friends, I like to see her, I acknowledge her importance to me, and I communicate it would be better for me if she called first to respect my time also. If she chose to take offense to what I said, I knew I could not control this. An important aspect of an assertive mindset is realizing you cannot control another person's behaviour. In this example I provided the information that I would like to be called first, that I care for her, and at the same time gave her room to respond how she chooses. There was no blame or shame attached, and the information I provided was information she could work with, as the information was relevant, truthful, and respectful.

Empathy is also about timing. For example if my friend had a bad day at work because she was left out of a birthday lunch, it might not be the best day to have this conversation. Nonetheless, if she had a terrible day and she showed up at my door and I really did not want to have a visitor I could say, "I understand you have had a bad day, however now is not a good time for me, could we talk about this tomorrow?" Which is also an example of asking for more time.

When preparing to have a more difficult conversation, it is good to set up a time with the other person, which is a way to respect both your time and the time of the person you want to have the conversation with. You could say something such as, "Hi Deborah, I want to talk to you about something that is very important to me, do you have time on Tuesday after work?" This communicates you want to have an important conversation, that the discussion is not something you want to speak of now, and it provides the other person an opportunity to consider when a good time for them would be to have an important conversation. If she asks what the conversation is about you could respond with, "It is a conversation that requires both our attention and it is important to me that we set time aside to discuss rather than discuss it now."

## *Scripting*

Above I was describing having a more difficult conversation that included using empathy, and also setting a time to discuss it. Scripting is another method you can utilize when you are preparing to have a difficult conversation. Scripting includes actually planning what you are going to say.

I once had an employee who was not performing at work and his attitude about work had soured noticeably. I went over numerous times how I would present what I have noticed to him and recited it over and over until I was confident in the delivery. Within the script, I incorporated other assertive techniques such as word choice, using "I" statements, and I even practiced my tone and body language for the delivery. I kept notes as well, which I brought to support me in case in the actual moment I clammed up. The result was that the delivery went very smoothly and he was quite understanding. He too noticed his own behaviour and owned up to it. He was also having some personal issues I was not aware of, but because of the delivery of the conversation, by thoughtfully scripting the conversation ahead of time, it gave me the confidence to have a difficult conversation, and maintain my focus throughout it. The notes supported me to keep me on track, as well as the practice. The employee did not respond in the ways I thought he would, yet I was prepared for possible reactions, such as what to do if he yelled, or blamed someone else, or what to do if he cried. The assertive techniques described in this book are tools you can use to support such scripting, and in how to respond to reactions of others. Although you cannot control how someone reacts, you can be prepared to respond in wise ways with the tools and techniques of assertive communication.

## *ABC*

The ABC is a form of a scripting as it is a formula you can use to prepare conversations. The formula is also easy to remember and use in unexpected situations. The ABC communication strategy is useful when dealing with street encounters, with employees not performing, with family members, or in any situation when a behaviour of someone else is not acceptable or respectful to you. The ABC strategy is a three step communication tool that clearly states what the problem is, how it affects you, and what you want the other person to do instead. The ABC formula consists of:

A: Directly state what the problem or issue is.

B: State how this affects you or the company.

C: State what you want that person to change or what you want to see from them moving forward.

**Example:** A person you do not know is catcalling[6] you, "Hey Hunny, look at your ass!"

You can respond to catcalling by saying:

A: "You in the blue shirt, I don't like being talked to like that."

---

[6]  Catcalling is being called at in a sexualizing manner, a form of unwanted verbal sexual attention.

B: "It makes me feel disrespected."

C: "From now on when you see me I want you to say hello Miss, or good day Miss"

**Example:** An employee has been late for three days in a row. As the manager you need to address this behaviour.

A: "I noticed you have been late three days in a row."

B: "It is important that you come to work on time as other employees need to go home, and by being late you make them late."

C: "Moving forward I ask you be on time, and if you cannot make it on time, please let me know thirty minutes prior to your shift."

If this is the first time the employee has shown being late as a new pattern, you might want to check in with the employee and find out if they are comfortable sharing with you the reason they are now coming in late. Maybe something is going on at home, or there has been a change in a daycare schedule. No matter what the reason, it is important to set a boundary for how you want them to address that behaviour.

## *Fogging*

When someone is blaming, questioning, or criticizing you in an aggressive way, fogging is a good tool to use. Fogging consists of identifying a piece of truth from what the person is throwing at you, agreeing with that part of what they are saying to you is true, and stating it back to them in a calm manner. It is important when using fogging to ignore any exaggerations and do not agree with or respond with what the person has accused you of that is not true.

For example, you have just come home and your partner is upset with you for being late.

Your partner exclaims, *"You are so late, how dare you keep me waiting!"*

You respond, *"Yes, I am late."*

*"I cannot believe you did not think to call me. I have been waiting."*

*"I am late. In hindsight I could have called you."*

*"Yes it was inconsiderate and I am upset."*

*"I see you are upset, and next time I will remember to call you."*

In the above example you are not denying or contesting what the person is saying. You are not being defensive. you are not criticizing them in turn. You are responding in a calm manner and you are not agreeing with everything the person is saying. You are only agreeing to what you see as truths from what the person has stated. The fogging response is like taking the hot stone the person is throwing at you, (the stone is the statement, accusation, or criticism that is meant to hurt you), and you catch the stone and respond to the stone by stating the truth in a calm tone, holding a grounded respectful stance, and thereby dissipating the emotional intensity. A fog occurs in nature when there is a warm or hot air that passes over a cool surface. The hot air is the emotional intensity behind the accusation, and by keeping cool and standing in your truth, you are what helps change the hot air into a calm fog versus perpetuating the hot air exchange.

Often times when people are accusing or criticizing they are upset and want you to be just as upset as them. Sometimes when people are hurt or feel wronged, they want you to feel hurt back. This is not the healthiest way to react. However, in relationships we are more able to be our raw vulnerable selves, and we show some of our less healthy developed parts of ourselves. When you take what is thrown at you, agree to part of it, and respond without defensiveness or heightened emotion, it reduces the energy of the accusation, criticism, or blaming, and the momentum slows down. Although in such an exchange you might feel heightened emotions, the trick is to use a calm voice, and deliver the responses with minimal emotional expression. When using fogging do not agree with any part of what the other person is saying that you do not actually think is true. Also do not agree to do what the other person is suggesting you do to repair how they have felt wronged, unless you truly agree you should.

Being assertive is about standing in your truth. If you were late, agree to the fact you were late. If you do not think it was inconsiderate, do not say you think you were inconsiderate. Use empathy here, think about your partner and their way of being. Some people get very riled about a person being late, if you know this, you might agree it was inconsiderate as it is prior knowledge you had of something that pushes your partners buttons and is seen as inconsiderate to them. However, even if your partner has buttons, it is not your job to skirt around them. Things happen in life that we do not always have control over, such as being late due to a road emergency blocking traffic. Being inconsiderate is pushing someone's buttons deliberately. Being inconsiderate is not experiencing an event outside of your control that happens to also push your partner's buttons. Your partner also has his or her own responsibility to work through their emotional triggers and discover ways to respond respectfully instead of react in ways that are aimed to increase your emotional upheaval and hurt you or others deliberately.

Responding with fogging is not a method from which you can expect changes in an abusive relationship where a partner may excessively question why you are late, where you have been, or who you were with. If you are in an abusive relationship and experience abusive or aggressive criticism and questioning, fogging might support you some of the time. However, living in an abusive relationship will wear you down. When you are worn down you might start to disbelieve yourself and your truth. Being assertive is also knowing when it is time to end a relationship, and learn information of how to end it safely. There are many resources to support ending unsafe relationships if you search the internet for domestic violence support, kids helpline, or you can talk to your doctor, or counsellor for help with developing a safety plan. If you are in immediate danger call 911.

Even in healthy relationships, interactions can become heated, and people can be angry at each other for seemingly unreasonable things. We each have a history of learning how to navigate life, and we each have our different triggers that can make us act from a less mature place. The idea of practicing assertiveness is to respond more maturely more often, and respond in a way that opens up opportunities for the people you are interacting with to also respond with maturity. If you came home late in the same interaction as the above example and responded defensively, it allows the argument to continue. When someone appears defensive it triggers a meme for the responding person to react either offensively or defensively depending on the person's behavioural programming.[7]

In fogging you do not need to explain yourself, unless you feel it is the best thing to do. Sometimes you are late for a reason, or sometimes you are just late. You do not have to give a reason, however below is an example of how to give a reason while using fogging without being defensive:

Spouse: *"You are so late. How dare you keep me waiting!"*

You: *"Yes I am late, there was an accident on 55th that held up traffic."*

---

7  A meme is a pattern of behaviour that is shared by most people in similar situation.

Spouse: *"I cannot believe you did not think to call me, I have been waiting."*
You: *"Yes I realize you have been waiting, however I was driving and it was unsafe for me to call."*
Spouse: *"It was inconsiderate and I am upset."*
You: *"I see you are upset, and the traffic was out of my control."*

In the example, in each response the assertive responder replies with something factual. Stating back words the other person has used supports reducing the momentum because when people hear back their own words, people feel heard. When people feel heard it can have a calming effect. Repeating the words back and saying, "I see you are upset", shows the person you are listening and acknowledging the persons' feelings, which is a form of empathy. When using fogging trust your intuition on what to say in response. The more you practice fogging, as like all the other skills in this book, the more easy it will be to use.

## *Responding to Compliments and Criticisms*

A part of assertiveness is also the ability to respond to compliments and criticisms. An odd, and normal, reaction people can have to receiving a compliment is feeling nervous, almost as if we do not believe the compliment to be true. Have you ever received a compliment and made an excuse for it?
Complementor: *"I love your hair today!"*
Responder: *"Well I barely brushed it and I really need a haircut."*
Accepting a compliment is something that can be done with practice and also supports confidence building. Accepting a compliment is agreeing with something positive someone says about you. How do you accept a compliment?

First, say a genuine thank you. Then ask, "What about that do you particularly like?"

Let's see this with the hair example:

Complementor: *"I love your hair today!"*

Responder: *"Thank you! What part of my hair do you particularly like?"*

Responding this way by asking to hear more about what the person is complimenting can feel awkward at first. However, accepting the compliment and asking for more specific information will grow your confidence because hearing positive things about yourself helps build positive affect. Accepting a compliment in this way helps build relationships as you find out more about the other person in your inquiry, such as what they like, and you enter into a more meaningful conversation.

Moving on to criticisms, if a criticism is coming from aggression, utilizing the fogging technique is a great strategy. However, not all criticisms are from aggression, and it can be tough to respond to even well meant constructive criticisms. When we are criticized a natural first response is defensiveness. Defensiveness closes off opportunities for improvement, and closes off communication. When someone constructively criticize you, a method for responding is accepting what you see is true, and asking further questions. For example, you cooked dinner and your spouse does not like it:

Spouse: *"Hunny, I don't like this dinner very much."*

You: *"It really is not that great is it. What part about it do you not like?"*

Spouse: *"It is very spicy."*

Another example: you are at work and your manager does not like the report you submitted.

Manager: *"The report is not good enough."*

You: *"Oh dear, what part of it needs improvement?"*

Manager: *"There are spelling mistakes throughout and I cannot follow the format clearly."*

You: *"Ok, let me take a look at it again and I will make some changes. I will forward you a new draft and if required, could we go over any further changes together?"*

Manager: *"Yes this will work."*

In each criticism it could be easy to take offense, and maybe you do feel offended. Nonetheless, despite your initial internal reaction it is important to respond in a calm manner and with honest inquiry to learn more about the reason for the criticism. What is it that needs improvement? Maybe you like the dinner really spicy and do not see an issue. However asking the question about what the other person does not like, gives you information you can build upon. Maybe you thought your report was amazing. However, questioning what needs improvement supports you in understanding what the other person sees. Assertiveness is gaining information so you can understand more about a situation. When you understand more, you can respond more wisely. Assertiveness is respecting the other person's point of view and at the same time respecting your own point of view. When you respond assertively to compliments and constructive criticisms it is a form of self-respect, and others will notice and will respect you more as well.

### Summary of Communication Techniques

Above are multiple communication techniques and skills to work with that will support your assertiveness practice. Some techniques will be easier for you to use than others, and other will take time and practice before they start working. When trying out the different skills and techniques you may be louder than normal, you may speak softer than normal, you may make mistakes, or you may use a technique that does not quite fit the situation. Practice anyway and keep trying. As you utilize the skills you will notice what works and what does not work in different situations. The more you practice assertive skills, the easier it will be to act more assertively in your life. The wisdom of which technique to use and when to use it effectively will also be easier over time.

# CHAPTER 11

## MORE ASSERTIVE SKILLS

Below are more assertive skills to support your practice. The below skills are more aligned with building your mind frame for your daily life as well as to support you in situations as you are choosing assertive communication.

### *Reframing*

Reframing is changing how you view a situation. Reframing can work when you are experiencing more negative (or unconstructive) emotions, as you can reframe these negative emotions as signals of a desire for change. When you are feeling badly about something, it is possible to see the bad thoughts and feelings as a sign to focus on what it is you really want instead of focusing on the feelings. For example, you just had an argument with a spouse and because of emotions it is very easy to focus on what is not working, what is wrong, or what he or she said instead of the golden nugget of what the emotion could be pointing toward. There is always a "what you want" within a "what you do not want" if you look for it (the golden nugget within the rock). Due to our well lived out emotion patterns and the subconscious doing the job of trying to keep us safe, most people go straight to focus on what is wrong in a situation. An awareness of what is wrong does have value as it is a signal we want something to change. However, when we sit in the "what is wrong" it does not support us. After a quick assessment of what it is you did not like or what was wrong in the argument, take the time to flip it, or reframe it, into the question, "What is it that I want in my relationship?" The reframe process is shown below.

Maybe what was wrong was:
*I do not want yelling*
*I do not like being blamed*
*I am tired of fighting*
*This argument never seems to end*
*We do not seem to understand one another*

And when considering what you want is (reframing):
*I want a joyful relationship*
*I want to be understood*
*I want healthy motivated inspiration from my relationship*
*I want clear communication*
*I want a deep understanding and connection in my relationship*

Notice how I did not use the term "I want better" in the reframing. When you use "I want better" in a reframe, or expect something to be better, you are not clearly defining what you want. This exercise has a built in reality check by acknowledging, "This is what I see and I do not like it," which is also an acceptance of what you are experiencing and how you feel about it. When you add the reframe of what you want into the reality check, "This is what I want to see and what I like," it is also an acceptance and an acknowledgment of how you feel about it. People are comparers by nature. It is part of our mental structure and function. Comparing one thing against another helps us make sense of our world, and helps us determine what different objects are in our reality by comparing the differences of objects, such as what a car is and a truck is. Part of what happens when people compare is we normally discount one thing over another, this is not a truck because it does not have a box at the back, or this is not happiness because I did not like what he said. We add value to what we compare as well, such as the following statements: "I am not happy therefore this situation is bad," (where as your happiness is more important than the situation) or, "A truck is better than a car." When we reframe by using "I want better," instead of clearly defining what we want, we will end up continually wish for something undefined that only exists in a future state. Better is not a definable concept because there can always be something better than what we have. What we want is what is important. What we want can also change as we gain more information. However, expressing what we want supports a concrete, definable, and working reframe rather than just expressing, "I want better." In our above exercise example, "clear communication" is better than "not understanding one another." Using "better understanding" does not give the mind a clear goal to strive for, whereas wanting "clear communication" gives your mind a direction to strive toward. Use this example to redefine your personal goals and point your mental compass to a place from which you can work toward.

## Story of Assertiveness

People are story tellers. We run story lines throughout our life about who we are, what we are good at, what we experience, how we feel about things, and what our dreams are. These story lines build our identity, how we see the world, how we see others, and how we see ourselves. The story lines we tell ourselves and others were built from our beliefs and experiences, and how we have perceived those experiences in the past. How we see things in the present moment is coloured by our feelings, thoughts, beliefs, and historical understanding of events in our lives.

When training others in assertiveness, I love bringing up the concept of stories because when a person realizes they are truly the author of their lives, they can change their narrative and their lives. Things happen to us that we did not write, such as if someone was in a car accident, that would not be their writing of the story. How they see the accident, how they interpret the meaning of it, and how they move forward from that experience would be an example of a story line they create.

Let us consider the story shared at the beginning of this book regarding the person who accosted my daughter and me. I could have hated strange men and built a distrust for all men I did not know. I could have racialized it. I could have believed that I am not safe to walk down the street ever again. The story I created is, I wanted to do something to learn how to respond if that situation ever occurred again. Crappy things happen to us in our lives including things we cannot control. The story concept is not about telling lies to yourself or painting the world with roses and rainbows (although you could if you wanted to). The story concept concerns working through some of the larger events that changed our lives or perceptions, do a reality check of what it really was, and form a story that will support you living the life you want.

Being accosted in a sexual way is something that happens to people. It does not happen to everyone but when it happens, it is not the targeted person's fault. It is a part of life that most of us find disturbing. Things like war, car accidents, and other forms of violence distress most people. These things exist and it hurts when they happen to us. Again, it is not the person's fault when another acts violently against them. When someone is violent against us, or hurts us intentionally, it is out of our control, and at the same time, it is a part of life. This is a reality check; Okay a very sucky reality check. Many times people think, "If only I listened to her. If only I did this instead. If only I was a better person. If only I did not dress that way. If only I did not trust him." These are stories framing the experiences as our fault. *Reality check.* When someone is violent against us it is not something we could have controlled at the time it happened. If it was up to us, it would not have happened at all.

When violence happens some people block it out. This is taking the story out of the story line. Some people blame themselves and live with the blame as long as they tell the story to themselves and others in a way that continues to point blame towards themselves. Some people minimize violence and say, "It was not like that." People sometimes minimize violence to help them cope with its existence in our lives and in the world. Any of these examples are personal stories, and are part of coping with a reality we do not like. When we face the fact that violence exists, it happens to people, and is not something the targeted person could have controlled, we can tell another story. I am discussing violence because the story of violence is meme one can easily be caught up in. A meme is a common understanding about an experience and people fall into similar patterns of behaviour around it. A common meme for experiencing violence is blaming the person who experiences the violence. Such comments as, "She should not have worn that," or, "He should not have been there," are examples of this. A person who experiences violence often blames themselves, believes they are a victim, and believes they are weak or unsafe because of some characteristic within themselves. This book is also being written to support persons who have experienced violence and have been victimized. There is a way out of this belief. Building confidence and self-esteem is a benefit of practicing assertive communication. Looking at what you want, instead of living out a meme, will support you in telling a story from which you can live free and no longer be victimized. Your story can incorporate that you are a stronger person as a result from the experience. An act of violence against me and my daughter opened up my story line of learning about physical assertiveness and building self-confidence through Karate, which then grew into a story of learning assertiveness and training others to learn and tell their own assertive story.

Here is an example of how framing stories can change how you experience your world. Please read the two stories below:

## Story #1

At work the other day I ran into a person who was upset. I asked her if she was okay and if anything was wrong and she said, "Nothing," in a short pointed tone and walked past me. I do not know what I did wrong and I thought about it all day. At the end of the day I saw her, and she was smiling and she waved goodbye to me.

## Story #2

At work the other day I ran into a person who was upset. I asked her if she was okay and if anything was wrong and she said, "Nothing," in a short pointed tone and walked past me. I care about people and did not know what was upsetting her but thought about her throughout the day and hoped she was okay. At the end of the day I saw her, and she was smiling and she waved goodbye to me.

What do you notice about these two stories? In the first story the observer is worried about all the things they cannot control and figured the other person was upset at something the observer had done, and she took on the responsibility for the other person's emotions. At the end of the day the other person was fine, suggesting the tone of the earlier encounter had nothing to do with the observer. In the second story, the observer did not take responsibility for the other person's emotions, and showed compassion for the other person. At the end of the day the observer received the information that the emotions of the other person were not personal. The observer in the second story had less stress throughout the day, and was able to focus on her day. The first observer was ruminating about what they did wrong to offend the upset person and spent more time in her day being stressed.

Our thoughts run stories in our heads to make sense of our reality on a regular basis, and with our imagination those stories can be based on assumptions or beliefs versus reality. When our stories are not supporting us, use any of the reality checks offered in this book, and ask yourself questions to discover the facts of the situation. You can shift the stories you tell into more supportive narratives that will help you build a healthy perspective and healthy self-esteem. Like everything else in this book, it takes practice.

Our brains respond to stories like it does the words we use. The stories we tell others and tell ourselves affect how we see the world and see ourselves, and literally formulate patterns in the brain on how we think and feel about ourselves and our world. Think about the stories you tell people on a regular basis. If you want to change your perspective, change your story. What are the stories you tell yourself? What is playing over and over again in your mind? Reflect on these. What do these stories communicate? What does your story of assertiveness look like?

## *Remember It is Not Personal*

Part of assertive training is not taking things personally. Although it is hard to realize that the person yelling at you, or acting emotional with you is not personal, there is more behind that person's feelings and actions. Emotional wisdom concepts lend support in situations where someone is yelling or being very emotional as you can use reframing techniques and also remind yourself that how someone reacts to you is not personal. People are responsible for their own emotions and actions. I see yelling as either a person feeling that they have no power other than to yell, or that they are feeling hurt themselves and yelling is a way to protect themselves. The next time someone yells at you, try seeing the act through one of these references and see how it changes how you are able to respond to the yelling.

## *Using Emotional Wisdom*

An entire section was dedicated to emotional wisdom theory and skills. I am mentioning it again here as emotional wisdom is an assertive skill. When using assertive communication skills there will be times when you feel you cannot respond due to your emotions. It takes courage to speak up for and from yourself. There are patterns people live out with family, authority, work, with strangers, and in friendships that sometimes make you feel you cannot be yourself or speak from yourself. Moving through and with emotions is one of the major challenges of practicing assertiveness, and is where implementing your new understanding of emotional wisdom and how the brain and psyche works will support you.

Assertiveness is also recognizing and accepting the reality of a situation. Sometimes things do not work out the way you want. Sometimes things are not the way you want. Sometimes there are things we cannot change. No matter what we are facing, we can change and choose our own perception. We can also change and choose our actions in regards to a situation. We cannot change someone else's perception and actions. We can offer information in hope of informing others of our intentions, wants, and needs. The more often we set our intention and show up assertively, the more clearer we are giving our information, and the more often we are understood and respected.

## Intuition

As discussed earlier, the world is made up of energy. Energy comes in many forms. We are forms of energy, and energy flows through us. Some people have a conscious awareness of their unconscious ability to feel and read different energies by tuning into different sensations in their bodies or other signals they learn to associate coming from their intuition. Feeling and reading energy is part of how intuition works. When my Grandma died, my Dad was climbing a mountain in New Zealand. He experienced a feeling that something was wrong while on the mountain and hiked down and called home as soon as he could. On that call he found out that Grandma had died. He somehow received information from energy that something had happened, something that was important, something big. He did not know exactly what it was, but he felt it, acknowledged it, and responded to it. This is intuition. This is not a super human power, this is a human power that we are all capable of.

Intuition can also occur in more regular situations. You meet someone and you have an off putting feeling about them. You cannot explain why but something is just off. Trust that feeling. Respond by keeping interactions short, distancing yourself, and trusting your intuition. If you are wrong, there is no harm done. If you are right, you might have saved yourself some serious heartache or from danger. I have experienced meeting someone and feeling off about them on first meeting, which I found out later was an intuitively correct assessment. I will share two of my experiences to display different outcomes of either listening or not listening to your intuition.

The experience in which I did not listen to my intuition and my initial feelings about a person, resulted in me allowing a person into my life that hurt me and others around me. When I first met this person my initial thought was, "Do not trust a word this person says," and I had a strong feeling of conviction about this thought. Despite this insight, I continued being around this person through social gatherings as he was integrated into a talking circle I was in. I then started to like him. He offered spiritual mastery and I was a person who sought to grow. I was attracted to spirituality at this time in my life. As it turned out, he was a completely untrustworthy person who was trying to control me, how I ate, and how I dressed, all under the guise that if I did these things I would become spiritually enlightened.

Why did I not listen to my intuition? Because I was moving away from myself. I had a belief that I was not spiritual or as powerful as he was, therefore I looked for answers through him and did not rely on or seek answers from myself. The truth was that my first intuition of him was one hundred percent accurate: "Do not trust a word this person says."

The time I did listen to my intuition was in a professional capacity. On first meeting, I did not trust this person. My intuition said, "Do not trust him." I had exercised assertiveness very well with this person. He would lie and not pay rent. I told him I thought he was being dishonest straight out when I noticed him lying. I asked him for information to support his story. He refused, and made excuses for why he could not provide it. I voiced to him that since he had not provided the information, I could not do what he was requesting. Each time he tried to distract me by blaming me or the institution for his issues. When he tried to demand something, I would refocus the conversations to the facts of the situation. It was found out later that this person would take as much as he could get from other people and companies by stealing and lying, and at the same time act like he was a victim. He placed the blame for his actions on everyone but himself. Some would label him a con artist. In the end he left, and the company I worked for did not lose a penny from him. I was assertive and trusted my intuition. I left the interactions with that person unharmed, although this person did harm a few other companies along his way.

Intuition is not always to warn you about harm. Intuition can give you a sense of trust for someone. The point is to do your best to learn how your personal intuition works, and practice listening to it and see the difference it can make in your life. If you make a mistake, you will know or it will become revealed in time. That is part of learning. Part of assertiveness is trying to utilize assertive skills. Listening to your intuition is one of the skills that will support you, and is a skill you can develop over time. Like all other assertive skills, it takes practice. When it does not work out after you have listened to or not listened to your intuition, try a different approach. The more you practice utilizing it, the more you will understand how your personal intuition works, and the more it will support you in your life.

# PART V

## FINALE

# CHAPTER 12

## LIVING ASSERTIVENESS
## TO THE FULLEST

By teaching assertiveness to others I learn even more about assertiveness from the people I work with. This is a practice that grows as there are endless scenarios of when choosing assertiveness supports the best outcome for all involved. I wrote this book to share my personal story of assertive growth, and to share the information that will support others in realizing the choice of assertiveness. Assertive communication and practice is a way of being that encourages others, shows the respect you have for yourself and the respect you have for others, and encourages confidence and esteem building. When people are confident and have healthy self-esteems, they are healthier people and act kindly and respectfully in the world. This is a world I want to be part of and help create in this lifetime.

# APPRECIATION

This book was written with inspiration from life, friends, family, and knowledge learned from studying social work, psychology, self-motivational works, and Emotional Wisdom Theory.[8] I am blessed to have learned from, and to have reframed my world with knowledge gained from my experiences and the people in my life. I continue to learn every day and encourage all who read this book to capture that spirit in their own lives. Learn to live a life assertively while also being appreciative of the opportunities that come along the way. We are all destined to grow, to be, and to realize our true selves. Like a flower, we blossom when we are given light; assertiveness is that light for me.

---

[8]  I learned about Emotional Wisdom Theory through various texts and working with Kate Michels who is founder of Core Alignment and the Emotional Wisdom Training Institute. To learn more please contact me through my website www.cherylfountain.com.

# ABOUT THE AUTHOR

Cheryl Fountain is a Core Alignment Coaching Specialist and Emotional Wisdom Trainer trained by Kate Michels, and has earned a Bachelor Degree in Social Work from the University of Regina, Canada. Cheryl is a third degree Reiki Practitioner, works with visualization techniques, is trained in Transpersonal Psychology, and has experienced more than 15 years as a professional business woman working with and within corporations. Her skills and experience support others in their journeys discovering their own unique potentials, and bringing more of their inner selves out and into the world. Cheryl grew up in Ontario Canada, and spent 17 of her years living in the Canadian Arctic. She followed her dream and moved closer to the Rocky Mountains, and now calls Alberta her home.

Check out Cheryl's website at

**www.cherylfountain.com**

cheryl fountain
light | communication | development

Thank you for reading! Please add a short review on Amazon and let me know what you thought!

Printed in Great Britain
by Amazon

25115678R00088